...ed in the UK in 1991 by
... (Publishers) Ltd
...ht Street, London W2 2AZ

...1992, 1994/1, 1994/2

...1991 in text, photographs and illustrations Barry Bier
...1991 New Holland (Publishers) Ltd

...served. No part of this publication may be reproduced,
...etrieval system or transmitted, in any form or by any
...ctronic, mechanical, photocopying, recording or otherwise,
... prior written permission of the copyright owners and publishers.

...68 144 X (hardback)
...868 226 8 (paperback)

...da de Villiers
...Robert Meas
...ign: Abdul Amien
...designs: Barry Bier
...Clarence Clarke
...phs: Juan Espi (pages 15, 29, 38, 45, 48, 53 and front and back cover)
...arbara McGregor
...eset by BellSet
...tion by Unifoto (Pty) Ltd
...nd bound in Singapore by Kyodo Printing Co (Pte) Ltd

BARRY B
THE ART
STAIN
GLASS
MADE EASY

This book is dedicated with love to the memory of my late son Mallarme and to my wife and life's companion, Anne Margaret.

NEW
HOLLAND

First publish
New Hollan
37 Connaug

Reprinted in

Copyright ©
Copyright ©

ISBN 1 85
ISBN 1 85

Editor: Lir
Designer:
Cover des
Template
Artwork:
Photogra
Stylist: E
Phototyp
Reprodu
Printed

All rights re
stored in a
means, ele
without th

CONTENTS

INTRODUCTION

Stained glass, or leaded light windows, have adorned buildings throughout the world for centuries. From the beginning of the Second World War, this fashionable art all but vanished until its world-wide revival in the 1970s. Renowned artists took to the medium and have created huge panels for airports and commercial buildings while many old windows, restored by skilled artisans, have become collector's items.

The oldest method used in this craft is the leaded type, followed by the copper foil technique, both requiring the cutting of many pieces of coloured glass with various textures and hard-to-cut surfaces. Once the glass has been cut, there follows the time-consuming activities of lead-cutting, assembling, soldering and puttying.

In this book, international artist Barry Bier introduces an exciting, new technique that does away with all these complicated and intricate procedures. Your designs can now be transferred onto single sheets of glass by applying adhesive and liquid lead and the different areas coloured in by means of special transparent glass paints, which are obtainable from craft shops worldwide. It's that simple – even a child can do it!

You will be able to produce beautiful stained glass objects, like those featured in this book, that will be virtually indistinguishable from traditional stained glass art – but at a quarter of the price and in much less time. There is no limit to what you can produce and you may be as ambitious as you wish – you can create stained glass windows for your home, an art deco lamp, a clock or a simple but delightful light-catcher to brighten a picture window. This new technique requires less skill but at the same time allows for greater creativity, giving many hours of happiness to the whole family.

Adhesive lead: This lightweight lead with a strong adhesive backing is available in 3 mm (1/8 in), 6 mm (1/4 in), 9 mm (3/8 in) and 12 mm (1/2 in) widths. The 3 mm (1/8 in) adhesive lead comes in 20 m (22 yd) rolls, while the others are available in 10 m (11 yd) rolls. For the best effect, use the 3 mm (1/8 in) width for small, elaborate objects.

Copper foil: This is available in various widths and if, for example, you are using 5 mm (3/16 in) thick glass, you will need 9 mm to 11 mm (3/8 in to 7/16 in) wide copper foil in order to allow for an overlap of 2 mm to 3 mm (1/16 in to 1/8 in) on either side of the glass. Before separate pieces of glass can be soldered together to form a single object, such as a vase, lamp, jewellery box and so on, the pieces must be surrounded by copper foil. A full description of this procedure is given with each project.

Detergent: An ammoniac-based cleaning detergent is required for cleaning the glass.

Felt-tip pen: Trace over your enlarged design with a fine-pointed felt-tip pen so that the design is clearly visible through the glass.

Flux: Available in liquid form, flux is applied sparingly to the copper foil before soldering as without it the solder will not adhere to the copper foil. It is not advisable to use resin or acid-core solder as the flux in this type of solder will eventually eat into the foil.

Frost texture: Available from art and hobby shops, transparent frost texture gives a lift to the stained glass object and can be used to create different effects, such as marbling, streaking, stippling and so on. Frosting also gives added protection to the finished stained glass object.

Glass: The most effective and the cheapest is 5 mm (3/16 in) clear glass. It is strong and, therefore, fairly difficult to break. However, for ceiling murals, wall murals or any object, such as a front door, which may be in danger of breaking, 4 mm (3/16 in) clear Perspex could be used. It is three to four times the price of glass, but it looks exactly the same.

Glass paints: Transparent glass paints are available in a variety of name brands and shades from art and hobby shops.

Knife: A lead or craft knife is required for cutting the adhesive lead.

Lacquer thinners: Available from hardware stores, these thinners are used to thin down the transparent glass paints.

Liquid lead: This is available in bottles and tubes and is used on the back of the designs.

Patina: This chemical solution is available from art and hobby shops and is applied to the soldered parts (which are silvery) on your stained glass object so that they blend in with the adhesive lead (which is grey). Patinas are available in black and copper as well. For instance, if a copper, rather than a lead effect is desired, the following steps are necessary: Wipe the adhesive lead with lacquer thinners. Brush the adhesive lead with flux and flow solder. Wipe again with lacquer thinners to remove the flux then, using a soft rag, rub copper patina over the soldered areas.

Pencils: Use an HB pencil to enlarge the designs or templates to the required size. If you are unsure of the correct colour selection, colour in the design using coloured pencils.

Sandstone: This is required for smoothing the edges of the glass once it has been cut.

Soldering iron and stick solder: You will need an 80–100 watt soldering iron and S/8 stick solder to solder some of the projects in this book, for instance the lamp (page 41), fruit bowl (page 49) and so on.

Yacht varnish: To protect the painted areas, a good, clear turpentine-based varnish must be applied to the painted and frosted areas and left to dry overnight.

Other materials: You will also need scissors, graph paper, an eraser, Tippex, pliers, masking tape, Prestik (Blu-Tack) and tracing paper.

TO PREPARE THE GLASS BEFORE USE

Once you have enlarged the template of your choice, ask your glass merchant to cut a piece of glass the size of your template. Before you can begin, the edges of the glass must be sanded and the glass washed thoroughly to remove dirt and grease.

1. Dip the sandstone in water and gently rub it along all the edges of the glass. Use a rag to hold and move the glass so as not to cut your hands. Once all the edges have been lightly rubbed, the glass is safe to handle. Most glass merchants should be able to sandstone the glass for you but it is more fun to do as much as possible yourself.

2. Dilute the detergent in a bucket or bowl of warm water and wash both sides of the glass thoroughly, then dry it with kitchen paper towel.

NOTE: *To clean Perspex, wash it in the ammoniac-based detergent and dry it with kitchen paper towel. Now spray the Perspex with an antistatic solution, which is available from chemists, and wipe dry with kitchen paper towel.*

ENLARGING THE DESIGN

If you do not have ready access to a photocopy machine that has enlarging facilities, use the grid system to enlarge your design. To do this you will need a sheet of graph paper, a pencil, a set square and a black felt-tip pen.

1. First decide how much larger you want the design to be. Using a felt-tip pen and a set square, draw a new grid of the correct size on the graph paper and label the squares as shown.

2. Now copy the design freehand onto the new grid, working one square at a time. Draw all the straight lines first, then fill in the curves and any other details.

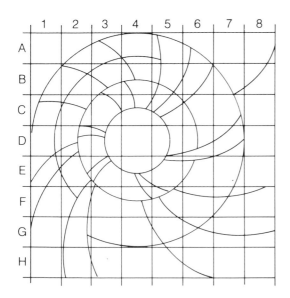

Grid system

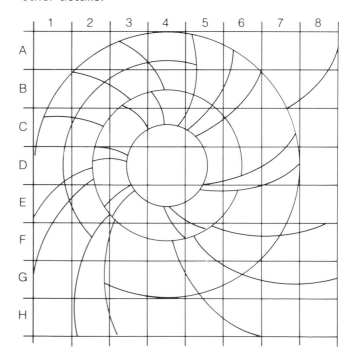

USING LIQUID LEAD

Practise on a piece of scrap glass before starting on your project. Place the nozzle directly on the glass and allow the lead to flow by itself. If it stops flowing, remove the bottle and clean the nozzle on a soft rag. Tilt the bottle once again and apply gentle pressure until the lead flows again. If working with 3 mm (1/8 in) wide adhesive lead, make sure that the hole in the nozzle of the liquid lead is small, but make it slightly bigger if using 6 mm (1/4 in) wide lead. Have a pin or a piece of thin wire ready to push into the nozzle to clear it of hardened lead.

USING ADHESIVE LEAD

Take your time before applying the lead and visualize where you will overlap one piece with another. Gently pull the lead to straighten it if it is twisted or bent. Always cut the shorter pieces, which are overlapped by longer pieces, at an angle. If you make a mistake, the lead can be easily lifted with your craft knife, and replaced.

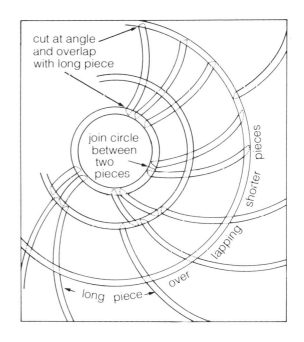

cut at angle and overlap with long piece

join circle between two pieces

shorter pieces

overlapping

long piece

NOTE: *Before applying adhesive or liquid lead, make sure the glass is warm, not cold. The warmth of your hands will make the cold glass damp and the lead will not stay glued. Place the glass near an electric heater for a short while to warm it up.*

USING TRANSPARENT GLASS PAINTS

These paints are available in a variety of exquisite, transparent colours as well as white, black and clear. It is important to use the same brand of paint when mixing different colours.

The consistency of these paints is relatively thick and the secret of this stained glass technique is to thin the paints before you begin painting. Dilute three parts paint with one part lacquer thinners. Although these paints take longer to dry once diluted, the paint flows more smoothly onto the glass and dries without bubbles or visible brush strokes. First experiment on a piece of scrap glass until you are satisfied that the paint runs smoothly. Don't make it too thin but rather flow a blob of paint onto the glass and wait a while to see that it settles and spreads to a smooth, even surface.

If you need *lighter* shades, add a few drops of colour to clear, mix the two paints together, adding more colour if necessary until you have the right shade. To make a colour more *opaque*, add a few drops of white to your colour, mixing it in with your paintbrush. This is particularly useful for shading petals or leaves, for instance.

To make *turquoise blue*, mix three parts blue with one part light green. To make *turquoise green*, mix three parts green with one part blue.

USING SOLDER AND A SOLDERING IRON

Before soldering your stained glass object, tape the copper-foiled sections together with masking tape. Apply flux sparingly in several places and put small drops of solder on the fluxed areas. (This is known as *spot* soldering.) These spots of solder can be easily removed with the soldering iron so that the pieces of glass can be adjusted if you are not satisfied with the fit. Now apply flux sparingly to all the seams (joints), and gently pull the soldering iron and solder along the copper-foiled seams. (This is known as *flow* soldering.)

WINDOWS OR DOORS

Turn a window or glass-panelled front door into a work of art by following these simple instructions. See pages 60-62 for templates.

THE METHOD

1. Measure the window pane you wish to replace with a stained glass one and buy a piece of glass that is 3 mm (1/8 in) smaller all round than this measurement. For example, if the window measures 200 mm x 300 mm (8 in x 12 in), buy a piece of glass measuring 194 mm x 294 mm (7¾ in x 11½ in). Cut the glass to size according to your template (or ask your glass merchant to do it for you) and gently sandstone the edges as described on page 6.

NOTE: *Remember to use a rag to hold and move the glass so as not to cut your hands. Once all the edges have been lightly rubbed, the glass will be safe to handle.*

2. Wash the glass with the ammoniac-based cleaning detergent, then dry it thoroughly with kitchen paper towel.

3. Enlarge the design of your choice onto a sheet of paper as described on page 6. If you have not decided on a colour scheme, colour in the design using pencil crayons which can be erased if you are not happy with the results.

4. Use masking tape to tape the design to your work surface, which should be covered with a blanket, and position the prepared glass on top. Use a piece of Prestik (Blu-Tack) on each corner of the glass to hold it in place.

5. Now follow the lines of the design with the adhesive lead (pull it off and adjust it if you are not following the lines accurately), overlapping pieces where necessary (see page 7).

NOTE: *For an interesting, three-dimensional effect use both 3 mm (1/8 in) and 6 mm (1/4 in) wide adhesive lead. Indicate on your design with a pencil which lines should have the 3 mm (1/8 in) wide adhesive lead and which the 6 mm (1/4 in).*

6. Turn the sheet of glass over and, following the lines of the adhesive lead, squeeze on the liquid lead. Apply even pressure and start at the top left-hand corner and work across and then down, so that there is no danger of smudging the wet liquid lead with your arm or hand. Wipe the nozzle of the tube or bottle on a rag before beginning each new line. Allow the lead to dry for at least two hours.

NOTE: *If you make a mistake, complete the liquid leading and allow it to dry. After about two hours, scrape off the offending line or smudge with your craft knife. Reapply the liquid lead and again allow it to dry thoroughly.*

7. Once the liquid lead is completely dry, wipe off any fingermarks on the glass with a soft rag and window cleaner.

8. Follow the instructions on using glass paints on page 7 and once you are happy with the shade and texture of each colour, begin painting, using the darkest colours first. Once again, begin at the top of the design and work downwards, remembering to allow each area to dry before painting an adjacent area. This is very important as the colour in one area may overflow and mix with the colour next to it. Clean your paintbrush thoroughly with thinners before using a new colour. Allow the completed design to dry for at least 24 hours.

9. Using a 4 cm (1½ in) or 5 cm (2 in) wide paintbrush, apply the transparent frost texture, smoothly and evenly, to the **painted** areas. Frosting takes from one to 10 hours to dry, depending on the room temperature, and will prevent the paintwork from getting scratched.

NOTE: *Transparent frost texture is ideal for creating different effects, such as stippling and marbling. Once dry, the frost texture is as clear as glass. Experiment on a piece of scrap glass and you will be surprised at what can be achieved.*

10. Once the frost texture has dried, thin down the yacht varnish with a little bit of turpentine thinners and carefully apply a coat to the painted areas. Allow to dry for 24 hours.

11. Ask an experienced glazier to install the window for you with the adhesive lead side of the window facing outward.

12. Once the window has been installed, use a soft rag to rub boiled linseed oil (available from hardware stores) over the lead. After a week, wash off the linseed oil with an ammoniac-based cleaner. Repeat this procedure at least twice a year to protect the lead from rain and sun.

LIGHT-CATCHERS

These delightful stained glass light-catchers will brighten up a sunny window. They are inexpensive and simple enough for a child to make.

THE METHOD

1. Enlarge the design of your choice (follow the instructions on page 6) or trace the template of your choice (pages 63-66) onto tracing paper and ask your glass merchant to cut a piece of glass the size of your template. Gently rub the edges of the glass with the sandstone.

NOTE: *Remember to use a rag to hold and move the glass so as not to cut your hands. Once all the edges have been lightly rubbed, the glass will be safe to handle.*

2. Wash the glass with the ammoniac-based cleaning detergent, then dry it thoroughly with kitchen paper towel.

3. Surround the sheet of glass with 10 mm to 12 mm (3⁄8 in to 1⁄2 in) wide copper foil as follows: Remove a small piece of the thin paper backing on the copper foil and, beginning at one corner, centre the copper foil along one edge of the glass. Slowly stick the copper foil all the way round the glass pane, until you reach the beginning, then overlap by 6 mm (1⁄4 in). (If you find the copper foil is not going on straight, pull it off and adjust it.) Using a piece of smooth wood, press along the entire length of the copper foil, then fold the edges over with your fingers. Press firmly to ensure that the foil sticks to the glass and then, using the piece of smooth wood, press along the entire length of both edges.

4. Using a black felt-tip pen, make a tracing of the design template on a piece of paper and, if you have not decided on a colour scheme, colour in the design using pencil crayons which can be erased if you are not happy with the results.

5. Use masking tape to tape the design to your work surface, which should be covered with a blanket, and position the prepared glass on top. Use a piece of Prestik (Blu-Tack) on each corner of the glass to hold it in place.

6. Now follow the lines of the design with the adhesive lead (pull it off and adjust it if you are not following the lines accurately), overlapping pieces where necessary (see page 7).

7. Turn the sheet of glass over and, following the lines of the adhesive lead, squeeze on the liquid lead. Apply even pressure and start at the top left-hand corner and work across and then down, so that there is no danger of smudging the wet liquid lead with your arm or hand. Wipe the nozzle of the tube or bottle on a rag before beginning each new line. Allow the lead to dry for at least two hours.

NOTE: *If you make a mistake, complete the liquid leading and allow it to dry. After about two hours, scrape off the offending line or smudge with your craft knife. Reapply the liquid lead and again allow it to dry thoroughly.*

8. Once the liquid lead is completely dry, wipe off any fingermarks on the glass with a soft rag and window cleaner.

9. Follow the instructions on using glass paints on page 7 and once you are happy with the shade and texture of each colour, begin painting, using the darkest colours first. Once again, begin at the top of the design and work downwards, remembering to allow each area to dry before painting an adjacent area. This is very important as the colour in one area may overflow and mix with the colour next to it. Clean your paintbrush thoroughly with thinners before using a new colour. Allow the completed design to dry for at least 24 hours.

10. Once the paint has dried completely, use your craft knife to scratch off any paint that may have got on the copper foil.

NOTE: *Transparent frost texture is ideal for creating different effects, such as stippling and marbling. Once dry, the frost texture is as clear as glass. Experiment on a piece of scrap glass and you will be surprised at what can be achieved.*

12. Once the frost texture has dried, thin down the yacht varnish with a little bit of turpentine thinners and carefully apply a coat to the painted areas. Allow to dry for 24 hours. If you have accidentally got varnish on the copper foil, scratch it off with your craft knife.

13. Make small loops from copper wire and attach them to the top two corners of the light-catcher with a drop of solder. Flow solder round the edge of the glass and along the loops themselves.

14. Using a soft rag, rub grey patina over the soldered areas so that they co-ordinate with the adhesive lead.

11. Using a 4 cm (1½ in) or 5 cm (2 in) wide paintbrush, apply the transparent frost texture, smoothly and evenly, to the **painted** areas. Frosting takes from one to 10 hours to dry, depending on the temperature, and will prevent the paintwork from getting scratched.

15. Attach a thin chain to the loops and hang the light-catcher in front of a sunny window.

JEWELLERY BOXES

Use the designs given on pages 67-69 or design your own. These lovely boxes make ideal gifts for friends and can be used to hold jewellery, cuff links or cigarettes.

THE METHOD

1. Enlarge the templates onto graph paper and ask your glass merchant to cut pieces of glass to measure. Gently sandstone the edges as described on page 6.

NOTE: *Remember to use a rag to hold and move the glass so as not to cut your hands. Once all the edges have been lightly rubbed, the glass will be safe to handle.*

2. Wash the pieces of glass with the ammoniac-based cleaning detergent, then dry them thoroughly with kitchen paper towel.

3. Surround each piece of glass with 10 mm to 12 mm (3⁄8 in to 1⁄2 in) wide copper foil as follows: Remove a small piece of the thin paper backing on the copper foil and, beginning at one corner, centre the copper foil along one edge of the glass. Slowly stick the copper foil all the way round the edge until you reach the beginning, then overlap by 6 mm (1⁄4 in). (If you find the copper foil is not going on straight, pull it off and adjust it.) Using a piece of smooth wood, press along the entire length of the copper foil, then fold the edges over with your fingers. Press firmly to ensure that the foil sticks to the glass and then, using the piece of smooth wood, press along the entire length of both edges.

4. Using a black felt-tip pen, make a tracing of the design template on a piece of paper and, if you have not decided on a colour scheme, colour in the design using pencil crayons which can be erased if you are not happy with the results.

5. Tape the design to your work surface, which should be covered with a blanket, and position the prepared glass on top. Use a piece of Prestik (Blu-Tack) on each corner to hold it in place.

6. Now follow the lines of the design with the adhesive lead (pull it off and adjust it if you are not following the lines accurately), overlapping pieces where necessary (see *Using adhesive lead* on page 7).

7. Turn each piece of glass over and, following the lines of the adhesive lead, squeeze on the liquid lead. Apply even pressure and start at the top left-hand corner and work across and then down, so that there is no danger of smudging the wet liquid lead with your arm or hand. Wipe the nozzle of the tube or bottle on a rag before beginning each new line. Allow to dry for at least two hours.

NOTE: *Transparent frost texture is ideal for creating different effects, such as stippling and marbling. Once dry, the frost texture is as clear as glass. Experiment on a piece of scrap glass and you will be surprised at what can be achieved.*

12. Once the frost texture has dried, thin down the yacht varnish with a little bit of turpentine thinners and carefully apply a coat to the painted areas. Allow to dry for 24 hours. If you have accidentally got varnish on the copper foil, scratch it off with your craft knife.

13. Using masking tape and leaving a 2 mm (1/16 in) gap between each piece of glass, stick the sides of the jewellery box together. Brush the copper-foiled corners with flux and spot solder (see page 7) all the joints.

14. When you are satisfied with the fit, remove the tape, brush flux along the copper-foiled edges and flow solder (see page 7) all the corner seams until the sides are completely soldered on the outside.

15. Brush flux onto the inner copper-foiled seams of the box and flow solder carefully so as not to get solder on the paint.

16. Turn the box over, tape the base in position and spot solder.

17. Remove the tape, brush the copper-foiled seams with flux and carefully flow solder the base to the sides.

18. Turn the box over, brush the inner seams with flux and flow solder carefully so that you don't get solder on the paint. Brush the copper-foiled edges of the lid with flux and flow solder right round the top edge of the lid as well.

19. Using a soft cloth, rub a little grey patina onto the silvery soldered areas so that they blend in with the adhesive lead.

NOTE: *If you make a mistake, complete the liquid leading and allow it to dry. After about two hours, scrape off the offending line or smudge with your craft knife. Reapply the liquid lead and again allow it to dry thoroughly.*

8. Once the liquid lead is completely dry, wipe off any fingermarks on the glass with a soft rag and window cleaner.

9. Follow the instructions on using glass paints on page 7 and once you are happy with the shade and texture of each colour, begin painting, using the darkest colours first. Once again, begin at the top of the design and work downwards, remembering to allow each area to dry before painting an adjacent area. This is very important as the colour in one area may overflow and mix with the colour next to it. Clean your paintbrush thoroughly with thinners before using a new colour. Allow the completed design to dry for at least 24 hours.

10. Once the paint has dried completely, use your lead or craft knife to scratch off any paint that may have got on the copper foil.

11. Using a narrow paintbrush, apply the transparent frost texture, smoothly and evenly, to the **painted** areas. Frosting takes from one to 10 hours to dry, depending on the temperature, and will prevent the paintwork from getting scratched.

WALL CLOCKS

You will need to buy a small box-type clock part (5.5 cm x 5 cm/2³⁄₁₆ in x 2 in) that runs on a tiny battery. Most small jewellery shops should stock the clock parts or will order one for you. Once the clock is complete, mount it in a wooden frame before attaching it to the wall.

THE METHOD

1. Enlarge the template on page 70 or 71 by following the instructions for *Enlarging the design* on page 6. Trace the template onto tracing paper and ask your glass merchant to cut a piece of glass to measure and to drill a 10 mm (³⁄₈ in) hole in the glass as indicated on the template.

2. Gently sandstone the edges as described on page 8.

NOTE: *Remember to use a rag to hold and move the glass so as not to cut your hands. Once all the edges have been lightly rubbed, the glass will be safe to handle.*

3. Wash the glass with the ammoniac-based cleaning detergent, then dry it thoroughly with kitchen paper towel.

4. Using a black felt-tip pen, make a tracing of the design template on a piece of paper and, if you have not decided on a colour scheme, colour in the design using pencil crayons.

5. Tape the design to your work surface, which should be covered with a blanket, and position the prepared glass on top. Use a piece of Prestik (Blu-Tack) on each corner to hold it in place.

6. Now stick 3 mm (¹⁄₈ in) wide adhesive lead along the lines of the design (pull the adhesive lead off and adjust it if you are not following the lines accurately), overlapping pieces where necessary (see *Using adhesive lead* on page 7).

7. Turn the glass over and, following the lines of the adhesive lead, squeeze on the liquid lead. Apply even pressure and start at the top left-hand corner and work across and then down, so that there is no danger of smudging the wet liquid lead with your arm or hand. Wipe the nozzle of the tube or bottle on a rag before beginning each new line. Allow to dry for at least two hours.

NOTE: *If you make a mistake, complete the liquid leading and allow it to dry. After about two hours, scrape off the offending line or smudge with your craft knife. Reapply the liquid lead and again allow it to dry thoroughly.*

8. Once the liquid lead is completely dry, wipe off any fingermarks on the glass with a soft rag and window cleaner.

9. Follow the instructions on using glass paints on page 7 and once you are happy with the shade and texture of each colour, begin painting, using the darkest colours first. Once again, begin at the top of the design and work downwards, remembering to allow each area to dry before painting an adjacent area. This is very important as the colour in one area may overflow and mix with the colour next to it. Clean your paintbrush thoroughly with thinners before using a new colour. Allow the paint to dry for 24 hours.

10. Using a 4 cm (1½ in) or 5 cm (2 in) wide paintbrush, apply the transparent frost texture, smoothly and evenly, to the **painted** areas. Frosting takes from one to 10 hours to dry, depending on the temperature, and will prevent the paintwork from getting scratched.

NOTE: *Transparent frost texture is ideal for creating different effects, such as stippling and marbling. Once dry, the frost texture is as clear as glass. Experiment on a piece of scrap glass and you will be surprised at what can be achieved.*

11. Once the frost texture has dried, thin down the yacht varnish with a little bit of turpentine thinners and carefully apply a coat to the painted areas. Allow to dry for 24 hours.

12. Screw in the clock face.

13. Mount the clock in a wooden or metal frame and attach it to the wall.

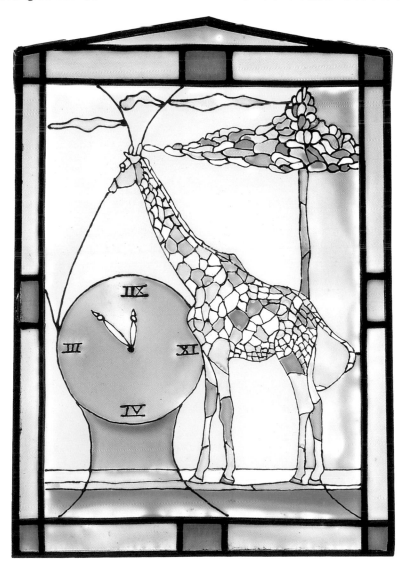

MIRRORS

Five different designs are provided on pages 72-75. Make a hanging mirror, standing mirror or hand mirror as an elegant gift for a special friend. As the hanging mirrors are fairly large, mount them in wooden or metal frames before hanging them on the wall.

THE METHOD

1. To make a wall mirror, follow the instructions on page 8 and enlarge the template on page 72 or 73 onto graph paper. Ask your glass merchant to cut a piece of glass and mirror to size.

2. Sandstone the edges of the glass and the front edge **only** of the mirror (see page 6).

NOTE: *Remember to use a rag to hold and move the glass so as not to cut your hands. Once all the edges have been lightly rubbed, the glass will be safe to handle.*

3. Wash the glass with the ammoniac-based cleaning detergent, then dry it thoroughly with kitchen paper towel.

4. Using a black felt-tip pen, make a tracing of the design template on a piece of paper and, if you have not decided on a colour scheme, colour in the design using pencil crayons which can be erased if you are not happy with the results.

5. Tape the design to your work surface, which should be covered with a blanket, and position the prepared glass on top. Use a piece of Prestik (Blu-Tack) on each corner to hold it in place.

6. Now follow the lines of the design with the adhesive lead (pull it off and adjust it if you are not following the lines accurately), overlapping pieces where necessary (see page 7).

7. Turn the glass over and, following the lines of the adhesive lead, squeeze on the liquid lead. Apply even pressure and start at the top left-hand corner and work across and then down, so that there is no danger of smudging the wet liquid lead with your arm or hand. Wipe the nozzle of the tube or bottle on a rag before beginning each new line. Allow to dry for at least two hours.

NOTE: *If you make a mistake, complete the liquid leading and allow it to dry. After about two hours, scrape off the offending line or smudge with your craft knife. Reapply the liquid lead and again allow it to dry thoroughly.*

8. Once the liquid lead is completely dry, wipe off any fingermarks on the glass with a soft rag and window cleaner.

9. Follow the instructions on using glass paints on page 7 and once you are happy with the shade and texture of each colour, begin painting, using the darkest colours first. Once again, begin at the top of the design and work downwards, remembering to allow each area to dry before painting an adjacent area. This is very important as the colour in one area may overflow and mix with the colour next to it. Clean your paintbrush thoroughly with thinners before using a new colour. Allow the completed design to dry for at least 24 hours.

10. Once the paint has dried completely, use your craft knife to scratch off any paint that may have got on the copper foil.

11. Using a 4 cm (1 1/2 in) or 5 cm (2 in) wide paintbrush, apply the transparent frost texture, smoothly and evenly, to the **painted** areas. Frosting takes from one to 10 hours to dry, depending on the temperature, and will prevent the paintwork from getting scratched.

NOTE: *Transparent frost texture is ideal for creating different effects, such as stippling and marbling. Once dry, the frost texture is as clear as glass. Experiment on a piece of scrap glass and you will be surprised at what can be achieved.*

12. Once the frost texture has dried, thin down the yacht varnish with a little bit of turpentine thinners and carefully apply a coat to the painted areas. Allow to dry for 24 hours.

13. With the adhesive lead side facing up, place the glass on top of the mirror. Use a piece of Prestik (Blu-Tack) in each corner to hold the mirror and the glass together and then fit them into a metal frame.

THE METHOD

1. *To make a standing mirror,* enlarge the templates on page 74 by following the instructions on page 6. Remember to enlarge the base and side pieces as well.

4. Surround the sheet of glass with 10 mm to 12 mm (3/8 in to 1/2 in) wide copper foil as follows: Remove a small piece of the thin paper backing on the copper foil and, beginning at one corner, centre the copper foil along one edge of the glass. Slowly stick the copper foil all the way round the glass pane, until you reach the beginning, then overlap by 6 mm (1/4 in). (If you find the copper foil is not going on straight, pull it off and adjust it.) Using a piece of smooth wood, press along the entire length of the copper foil, then fold the edges over with your fingers. Press firmly to ensure that the foil sticks to the glass and then, using the piece of smooth wood, press along the entire length of both edges. Repeat this procedure with the mirror.

5. Follow Steps 5-12 for the wall mirror.

NOTE: *If you got varnish on the copper foil, scratch it off with your craft knife.*

6. Place the mirror on your work surface and position the painted glass, adhesive lead side up, on top. Using masking tape, tape the two pieces together securely.

7. Brush flux on the corners and, with the two pieces lying flat and on the edge of your work surface, spot solder.

NOTE: *It is very important that you do not hold the two pieces upright when fluxing and soldering as the flux and solder will run between the mirror and the glass and ruin the effect.*

8. When you are happy with the fit, remove the tape, brush flux sparingly on the copper foil and flow solder (page 7) round the edges of the glass and the mirror.

9. Using masking tape, tape the base and side pieces to the glass. When you are happy with the fit, brush flux on the corners and spot solder. Remove the tape, brush flux along the outer seams and flow solder. Brush flux along the inner seams and flow solder again.

2. Cut the glass and mirror to size according to your template (or ask your glass merchant to do it for you) and gently sandstone the edges of the glass as described on page 8.

NOTE: *Remember to use a rag to hold and move the glass so as not to cut your hands. Once all the edges have been lightly rubbed, the glass will be safe to handle.*

3. Wash the glass with the ammoniac-based cleaning detergent, then dry it thoroughly with kitchen paper towel.

1. *To make the hand mirror*, enlarge the template on page 75 and ask your glass merchant to cut a piece of glass and a mirror the same size as your template.

2. Gently sandstone the edges of the glass and the front edge only of the mirror as described on page 6.

NOTE: *Remember to use a rag to hold and move the glass so as not to cut your hands. Once all the edges have been lightly rubbed, the glass will be safe to handle.*

3. Wash the glass and mirror with the ammoniac-based cleaning detergent, then dry them thoroughly with kitchen paper towel.

4. Surround the piece of glass with 10 mm to 12 mm (3/8 in to 1/2 in) wide copper foil as follows: Remove a small piece of the thin paper backing on the copper foil and, beginning at one corner, centre the copper foil along one edge of the glass. Slowly stick the copper foil all the way round the glass pane, until you reach the beginning, then overlap by 6 mm (1/4 in). (If you find the copper foil is not going on straight, pull it off and adjust it.) Using a piece of smooth wood, press along the entire length of the copper foil, then fold the edges over with your fingers. Press firmly to ensure that the foil sticks to the glass and then, using the piece of smooth wood, press along the entire length of both edges. Repeat this procedure with the mirror.

5. Using a black felt-tip pen, make a tracing of the design template on a piece of paper and, if you have not decided on a colour scheme, colour in the design using pencil crayons which can be erased if you are not happy with the results.

6. Tape the design template to your work surface, which should be covered with a blanket, and position the prepared glass on top. Use pieces of Prestik (Blu-Tack) to hold the glass in place.

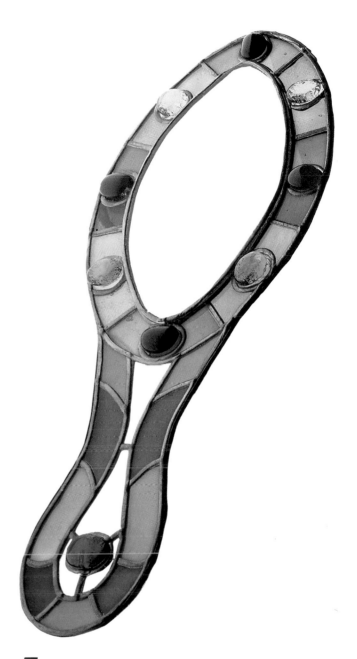

7. Now follow the lines of the design with the adhesive lead (pull it off and adjust it if you are not following the lines accurately), overlapping pieces where necessary (see page 7).

8. Turn the sheet of glass over and, following the lines of the adhesive lead, squeeze on the liquid lead. Apply even pressure and start at the top left-hand corner and work across and then down, so that there is no danger of smudging the wet liquid lead with your arm or hand. Wipe the nozzle of the tube or bottle on a rag before beginning each new line. Allow to dry for at least two hours.

NOTE: *If you make a mistake, complete the liquid leading and allow it to dry. After about two hours, scrape off the offending line or smudge with your craft knife. Reapply the liquid lead and again allow it to dry thoroughly.*

9. Once the liquid lead is completely dry, wipe off any fingermarks on the glass with a soft rag and window cleaner.

10. Follow the instructions on using glass paints on page 7 and once you are happy with the shade and texture of each colour, begin painting, using the darkest colours first. Once again, begin at the top of the design and work downwards, remembering to allow each area to dry before painting an adjacent area. This is very important as the colour in one area may overflow and mix with the colour next to it. Clean your paintbrush thoroughly with thinners before using a new colour. If you have difficulty finding the coloured glass stones, as shown in the photograph, or prefer to omit them, these areas can be painted. Allow the completed design to dry for 24 hours.

11. Once the paint has dried completely, use your craft knife to scratch off any paint that may have got on the copper foil.

12. Using a paintbrush, apply the transparent frost texture, smoothly and evenly, to the **painted** areas. Frosting takes from one to 10 hours to dry, depending on the temperature, and will prevent the paintwork from getting scratched.

NOTE: *Transparent frost texture is ideal for creating different effects, such as stippling and marbling. Once dry, the frost texture is as clear as glass. Experiment on a piece of scrap glass and you will be surprised at what can be achieved.*

13. Once the frost texture has dried, thin down the yacht varnish with a little bit of turpentine thinners and carefully apply a coat to the painted areas. Allow to dry for 24 hours. If you have accidentally got varnish on the copper foil, scratch it off with your craft knife.

14. With the adhesive lead side of the glass on top, tape the mirror to the back of the glass. With the two pieces lying flat and on the edge of your work surface, brush flux in about six different places round the edge of the mirror and glass and spot solder to secure the two sections. Remove the tape, brush flux along the copper-foiled seam and flow solder right round.

NOTE: *It is very important that you do not hold the two pieces upright when fluxing and soldering as the flux and solder will run between the mirror and the glass and ruin the effect.*

15. If you are using the coloured glass stones, glue them in position.

16. Using a soft rag, rub grey patina on the silvery soldered areas to match the grey of the adhesive lead.

BAR SIGNS

Use either of the designs on page 76 or design your own sign to brighten up a home pub.

THE METHOD

1. Decide how large you want the bar sign to be and enlarge the template on graph paper by following the instructions on page 6. Cut the glass to size according to your template (or ask your glass merchant to do it for you) and gently sandstone the edges as described on page 6.

NOTE: *Remember to use a rag to hold and move the glass so as not to cut your hands. Once all the edges have been lightly rubbed, the glass will be safe to handle.*

2. Wash the glass with the ammoniac-based cleaning detergent, then dry it thoroughly with kitchen paper towel.

3. Using a black felt-tip pen, make a tracing of the design template on a piece of paper and, if you have not decided on a colour scheme, colour in the design using pencil crayons which can be erased if you are not happy with the results.

4. Use masking tape to tape the design to your work surface, which should be covered with a blanket, and position the prepared glass on top. Use a piece of Prestik (Blu-Tack) on each corner of the glass to hold it in place.

5. Now follow the lines of the design with the adhesive lead (pull it off and adjust it if you are not following the lines accurately), overlapping pieces where necessary (see page 7).

NOTE: *For an interesting, three-dimensional effect, use both 3 mm (1/8 in) and 6 mm (1/4 in) wide adhesive lead. Indicate on your design with a pencil which lines should have the 3 mm (1/8 in) adhesive lead and which the 6 mm (1/4 in).*

6. Turn the sheet of glass over and, following the lines of the adhesive lead, squeeze on the liquid lead. Apply even pressure and start at the top left-hand corner and work across and then down, so that there is no danger of smudging the wet liquid lead with your arm or hand. Wipe the nozzle of the tube or bottle on a rag before beginning each new line. Allow to dry for at least two hours.

NOTE: *If you make a mistake, complete the liquid leading and allow it to dry. After about two hours, scrape off the offending line or smudge with your lead or craft knife. Reapply the liquid lead and again allow it to dry thoroughly.*

7. Once the liquid lead is completely dry, wipe off any fingermarks on the glass with a soft rag and window cleaner.

8. Follow the instructions on using glass paints on page 7 and once you are happy with the shade and texture of each colour, begin painting, using the darkest colours first. Once again, begin at the top of the design and work downwards, remembering to allow each area to dry before painting an adjacent area. This is very important as the colour in one area may overflow and mix with the colour next to it. Clean your paintbrush thoroughly with thinners before using a new colour. Allow the paint to dry for 24 hours.

9. Using a 4 cm (1 ½ in) or 5 cm (2 in) wide paintbrush, apply the transparent frost texture, smoothly and evenly, to the **painted** areas. Frosting takes from one to 10 hours to dry, depending on the temperature, and will prevent the paintwork from getting scratched.

NOTE: *Transparent frost texture is ideal for creating different effects, such as stippling and marbling. Once dry, the frost texture is as clear as glass. Experiment on a piece of scrap glass and you will be surprised at what can be achieved.*

10. Once the frost texture has dried, thin down the yacht varnish with a little bit of turpentine thinners and carefully apply a coat to the painted areas. Allow to dry for 24 hours.

11. Mount the bar sign, adhesive lead side in front, in a deep wooden frame. Hang the sign above or behind the bar and position a spotlight or fluorescent light behind the sign to light up the stained glass design.

WELCOME SIGNS

Hang one of these signs in your window or on your glass-panelled front door to welcome your friends to your home.

THE METHOD

1. Enlarge the template on page 77 on graph paper, following the instructions on page 6. Cut the glass to size according to your template and gently sandstone the edges as described on page 6.

NOTE: *Remember to use a rag to hold and move the glass so as not to cut your hands. Once all the edges have been lightly rubbed, the glass will be safe to handle.*

2. Wash the glass with the ammoniac-based cleaning detergent, then dry it thoroughly with kitchen paper towel.

3. Surround the sheet of glass with 10 mm to 12 mm (⅜ in to ½ in) wide copper foil as follows: Remove a small piece of the thin paper backing on the copper foil and, beginning at one corner, centre the copper foil along one edge of the glass. Slowly stick the copper foil all the way round the

glass pane until you reach the beginning, then overlap by 6 mm (¼ in). If you find the copper foil is not going on straight, pull it off and adjust it.) Using a piece of smooth wood, press along the entire length of the copper foil, then fold the edges over with your fingers. Press firmly to ensure that the foil sticks to the glass and then, using the piece of smooth wood, press along the entire length of both edges.

4. Using a black felt-tip pen, make a tracing of the design template on a piece of paper and, if you have not decided on a colour scheme, colour in the design using pencil crayons which can be erased if you are not happy with the results.

5. Tape the design template to your work surface, which should be covered with a blanket, and position the prepared glass on top. Use a piece of Prestik (Blu-Tack) on each corner of the glass to hold it in place.

6. Now follow the lines of the design with the adhesive lead (pull it off and adjust it if you are not following the lines accurately), overlapping pieces where necessary (see page 7).

NOTE: *For an interesting, three-dimensional effect use both 3 mm (1/8 in) and 6 mm (1/4 in) wide adhesive lead. Indicate on your design with a pencil which lines should have the 3 mm (1/8 in) adhesive lead and which the 6 mm (1/4 in).*

7. Turn the sheet of glass over and, following the lines of the adhesive lead, squeeze on the liquid lead. Apply even pressure and start at the top left-hand corner and work across and then down, so that there is no danger of smudging the wet liquid lead with your arm or hand. Wipe the nozzle of the tube or bottle on a rag before beginning each new line. Allow to dry for at least two hours.

NOTE: *If you make a mistake, complete the liquid leading and allow it to dry. After about two hours, scrape off the offending line or smudge with your lead or craft knife. Reapply the liquid lead and again allow it to dry thoroughly.*

8. Once the liquid lead is completely dry, wipe off any fingermarks on the glass with a soft rag and window cleaner.

9. Follow the instructions on using glass paints on page 7 and once you are happy with the shade and texture of each colour, begin painting, using the darkest colours first. Once again, begin at the top of the design and work downwards, remembering to allow each area to dry before painting an adjacent area. This is very important as the colour in one area may overflow and mix with the colour next to it. Clean your paintbrush thoroughly with thinners before using a new colour. Allow the completed design to dry for at least 24 hours.

10. Once the paint has dried completely, use your lead or craft knife to scratch off any paint that may have got onto the copper foil.

11. Using a 4 cm (1 1/2 in) or 5 cm (2 in) wide paintbrush, apply the transparent frost texture, smoothly and evenly, to the painted areas. Frosting takes from one to 10 hours to dry, depending on the temperature, and will prevent the paintwork from getting scratched.

NOTE: *Transparent frost texture is ideal for creating different effects, such as stippling and marbling. Once dry, the frost texture is as clear as glass. Experiment on a piece of scrap glass and you will be surprised at what can be achieved.*

12. Once the frost texture has dried, thin down the yacht varnish with a little bit of turpentine thinners and carefully apply a coat to the painted areas. Allow to dry for 24 hours. If you have accidentally got varnish on the copper foil, scratch it off with your craft knife.

13. Brush the copper foil with flux and flow solder round the edge of the glass. Using a soft rag, rub grey patina over the soldered areas so as to coordinate with the leaded areas.

14. Make small loops from copper wire and attach them to the top two corners of the sign with a drop of solder. Attach a chain and hang the welcome sign with the adhesive lead side of the glass facing the approaching visitors.

NOTE: *Alternatively, omit Step 3 and mount the welcome sign, adhesive lead side facing out, in a deep wooden frame with sufficient space behind it to accommodate a light bulb.*

HOUSE NUMBERS

All the numerals you require can be found on page 79. Use the designs featured on page 78 and substitute the numerals with your own house number.

THE METHOD

1. Enlarge the template on graph paper, following the instructions on page 6. Cut the glass to size according to your template (or ask your glass merchant to do it for you) and gently sandstone the edges as described on page 6.

NOTE: *Remember to use a rag to hold and move the glass so as not to cut your hands. Once all the edges have been lightly rubbed, the glass will be safe to handle.*

2. Wash the glass with the ammoniac-based cleaning detergent, then dry it thoroughly with kitchen paper towel.

3. Surround the sheet of glass with 10 mm to 12 mm (³⁄₈ in to ¹⁄₂ in) wide copper foil as follows: Remove a small piece of the thin paper backing on the copper foil and, beginning at one corner, centre the copper foil along one edge of the glass. Slowly stick the copper foil all the way round the glass pane, until you reach the beginning, then overlap by 6 mm (¹⁄₄ in). (If you find the copper foil is not going on straight, pull it off and adjust it.) Using a piece of smooth wood, press along the entire length of the copper foil, then fold the edges over with your fingers. Press firmly to ensure that the foil sticks to the glass and then, using the piece of smooth wood, press along the entire length of both edges.

4. Using a black felt-tip pen, make a tracing of the design template on a piece of paper and, if you have not decided on a colour scheme, colour in the design using pencil crayons which can be erased if you are not happy with the results.

5. Tape the design template to your work surface, which should be covered with a blanket, and position the prepared glass on top. Use a piece of Prestik (Blu-Tack) on each corner of the glass to hold it in place.

6. Now follow the lines of the design with the adhesive lead (pull it off and adjust it if you are not following the lines accurately), overlapping pieces where necessary (see page 7).

NOTE: *For an interesting, three-dimensional effect use both 3 mm (¹⁄₈ in) and 6 mm (¹⁄₄ in) wide adhesive lead. Indicate on your design with a pencil which lines should have the 3 mm (¹⁄₈ in) adhesive lead and which the 6 mm (¹⁄₄ in).*

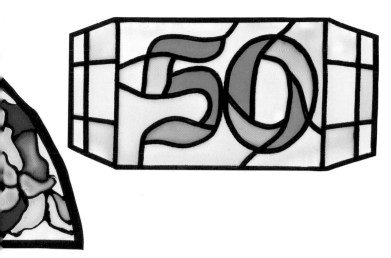

9. Follow the instructions on using glass paints on page 7 and once you are happy with the shade and texture of each colour, begin painting, using the darkest colours first. Once again, begin at the top of the design and work downward, remembering to allow each area to dry before painting an adjacent area. This is very important as the colour in one area may overflow and mix with the colour next to it. Clean your paintbrush thoroughly with thinners before using a new colour. Allow the paint to dry for 24 hours.

10. Once the paint has dried completely, use your lead or craft knife to scratch off any paint that may have got onto the copper foil.

11. Using a 4 cm (1½ in) or 5 cm (2 in) wide paintbrush, apply the transparent frost texture, smoothly and evenly, to the **painted** areas. Frosting takes from one to 10 hours to dry, depending on the temperature, and will prevent the paintwork from getting scratched.

NOTE: *Transparent frost texture is ideal for creating different effects, such as stippling and marbling. Once dry, the frost texture is as clear as glass. Experiment on a piece of scrap glass and you will be surprised at what can be achieved.*

12. Once the frost texture has dried, thin down the yacht varnish with a little bit of turpentine thinners and carefully apply a coat to the painted areas. Allow to dry for 24 hours. If you have accidentally got varnish on the copper foil, scratch it off with your craft knife.

13. Brush flux on the copper foil and flow solder round the edge of the glass. Using a soft rag, rub grey patina over the soldered areas so as to co-ordinate with the leaded areas.

14. Make small loops from copper wire and attach them to the top two corners with a drop of solder. Attach a chain to hang the house number.

NOTE: *Alternatively, omit Step 3 and mount your house number in a deep wooden frame with sufficient space behind it for a light bulb.*

7. Turn the sheet of glass over and, following the lines of the adhesive lead, squeeze on the liquid lead. Apply even pressure and start at the top left-hand corner and work across and then down, so that there is no danger of smudging the wet liquid lead with your arm or hand. Wipe the nozzle of the tube or bottle on a rag before beginning each new line. Allow to dry for at least two hours.

NOTE: *If you make a mistake, complete the liquid leading and allow it to dry. After about two hours, scrape off the offending line or smudge with your craft knife. Reapply the liquid lead and again allow it to dry thoroughly.*

8. Once the liquid lead is completely dry, wipe off any fingermarks on the glass with a soft rag and window cleaner.

PICTURE FRAMES

Make these picture frames and use them to show off your family photographs. Templates for a hanging frame and two standing frames can be found on page 80.

THE METHOD

1. Enlarge the template on graph paper, following the instructions on page 6. Cut the glass to size according to your template (or ask your glass merchant to do it for you). If you are making the *standing frame*, remember to enlarge the base and two side pieces proportionately and have pieces of glass cut to size. Gently sandstone the edges as described on page 6.

NOTE: *Remember to use a rag to hold and move the glass so as not to cut your hands. Once all the edges have been lightly rubbed, the glass will be safe to handle.*

2. Wash the glass with the ammoniac-based cleaning detergent, then dry it thoroughly with kitchen paper towel.

3. Surround the sheet of glass with 10 mm to 12 mm (3⁄8 in to 1⁄2 in) wide copper foil as follows: Remove a small piece of the thin paper backing on the copper foil and, beginning at one corner, centre the copper foil along one edge of the glass. Slowly stick the copper foil all the way round the glass pane, until you reach the beginning, then overlap by 6 mm (1⁄4 in). (If you find the copper foil is not going on straight, pull it off and adjust it.) Using a piece of smooth wood, press along the entire length of the copper foil, then fold the edges over with your fingers. Press firmly to ensure that the foil sticks to the glass and then, using the piece of smooth wood, press along the entire length of both edges.

4. Using a black felt-tip pen, make a tracing of the design template on a piece of paper and, if

you have not decided on a colour scheme, colour in the design using pencil crayons which can be erased if you are not happy with the results.

5. Tape the design template to your work surface, which should be covered with a blanket, and position the prepared glass on top. Use a piece of Prestik (Blu-Tack) on each corner of the glass to hold it in place.

6. Follow the lines of the design with the adhesive lead (pull it off and adjust it if you are not following the lines accurately), overlapping pieces where necessary (see page 7).

7. Turn the sheet of glass over and, following the lines of the adhesive lead, squeeze on the liquid lead. Apply even pressure and start at the top left-hand corner and work across and then down, so that there is no danger of smudging the wet liquid lead with your arm or hand. Wipe the nozzle of the tube or bottle on a rag before beginning each new line. Allow to dry for at least two hours.

NOTE: *If you make a mistake, complete the liquid leading and allow it to dry. After about two hours, scrape off the offending line or smudge with your craft knife. Reapply the liquid lead and again allow it to dry thoroughly.*

8. Once the liquid lead is completely dry, wipe off any fingermarks on the glass with a soft rag and window cleaner.

9. Follow the instructions on using glass paints on page 7 and once you are happy with the shade and texture of each colour, begin painting, using the darkest colours first. Begin at the top of the design and work downward, remembering to allow each area to dry before painting an adjacent area as the colour in one area may overflow and mix with the colour next to it. Clean your paintbrush with thinners before using a new colour. Allow the paint to dry for 24 hours.

10. When the paint is completely dry, scratch off any paint that may have got on the copper foil.

11. Using a small paintbrush, apply the transparent frost texture, smoothly and evenly, to the **painted** areas. Frosting takes from one to 10 hours to dry, depending on the temperature, and will prevent the paintwork from getting scratched.

NOTE: *Transparent frost texture is ideal for creating different effects, such as stippling and marbling. Once dry, the frost texture is as clear as glass. Experiment on a piece of scrap glass and you will be surprised at what can be achieved.*

12. Once the frost texture has dried, thin down the yacht varnish with a little bit of turpentine thinners and carefully apply a coat to the painted areas. Allow to dry for 24 hours. If you have accidentally got varnish on the copper foil, scratch it off with your craft knife.

13. *For the hanging frame*, brush the copper foil with flux and flow solder round the edge of the glass. Make small loops from copper wire and attach them to the top two corners with a drop of solder. Attach a thin chain to the loops so that the picture frame can be hung on a wall.

14. Using a soft rag, rub grey patina over the soldered areas so that they blend in with the leaded areas.

NOTE: *Alternatively, omit Step 3 and 13 and mount the glass in a wooden or metal frame.*

15. *For the standing frames*, apply copper foil to the edges of the base and side pieces, then tape them to the frame. When you are happy with the fit and the frame stands correctly, position the frame flat over the edge of your work surface, brush sparingly with flux and spot solder the base and the side pieces to the frame. Remove the tape, brush flux along the seams and flow solder along the outer seams and then the inner seams.

NOTE: *It is very important that you do not hold the pieces upright when fluxing and soldering as the flux and solder may run between the glass and the base and side pieces and ruin the effect.*

16. Using a soft rag, rub grey patina over the soldered areas so that they blend in with the adhesive lead.

17. Brush clear glue on the back of your photograph to within 6 mm (¼ in) from the edges. Let the glue dry for 30 seconds before positioning the photograph neatly in the centre of the frame.

MOBILE

These colourful birds make a delightful mobile for a child's room. Templates can be found on pages 81 and 82.

THE METHOD

1. Enlarge the templates on graph paper, following the instructions on page 6, and cut the glass to size according to your templates (or ask your glass merchant to do it for you). Gently sandstone the edges as described on page 6.

NOTE: *Remember to use a rag to hold and move the glass so as not to cut your hands. Once all the edges have been lightly rubbed, the glass will be safe to handle.*

2. Wash the pieces of glass with the ammoniac-based cleaning detergent, then dry them thoroughly with kitchen paper towel.

3. Surround each piece of glass with 10 mm to 12 mm (3/8 in to 1/2 in) wide copper foil as follows: Remove a small piece of the thin paper backing on the copper foil and, beginning at one corner, centre the copper foil along one edge of the glass. Slowly stick the copper foil all the way round the glass, until you reach the beginning, then overlap by 6 mm (1/4 in). (If you find the copper foil is not going on straight, pull it off and adjust it.) Using a piece of smooth wood, press along the entire length of the copper foil, then fold the edges over with your fingers. Press firmly to ensure that the foil sticks to the glass and then, using the piece of smooth wood, press along the entire length of both edges.

4. Using a black felt-tip pen, make a tracing of the design template on a piece of paper and, if you have not decided on a colour scheme, colour in the design using pencil crayons which can be erased if you are not happy with the results.

5. Tape each design to your work surface, which should be covered with a blanket, and position the prepared glass on top. Use a piece of Prestik (Blu-Tack) on each corner of the glass to hold it firmly in place.

6. Now, follow the lines of the design with the lead (pull it off and adjust it if you are not following the lines accurately), overlapping pieces where necessary (see page 7).

7. Turn the pieces of glass over and, following the lines of the adhesive lead, squeeze on the liquid lead. Apply even pressure and start at the top left-hand corner and work across and then down, so that there is no danger of smudging the wet liquid lead with your arm or hand. Wipe the nozzle of the tube or bottle on a rag before beginning each new line. Allow to dry for at least two hours.

NOTE: *If you make a mistake, complete the liquid leading and allow it to dry. After about two hours, scrape off the offending line or smudge with your craft knife. Reapply the liquid lead and again allow it to dry thoroughly.*

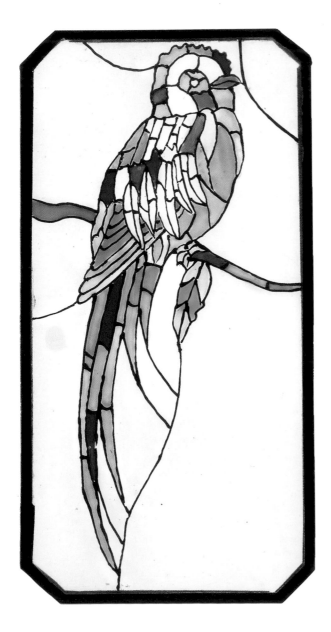

8. Once the liquid lead is completely dry, wipe off any fingermarks on the glass with a soft rag and window cleaner.

9. Follow the instructions on using glass paints on page 7 and once you are happy with the shade and texture of each colour, begin painting, using the darkest colours first. Once again, begin at the top of each design and work downward, remembering to allow each area to dry before painting an adjacent area. This is very important as the colour in one area may overflow and mix with the colour next to it. Clean your paintbrush thoroughly with thinners before using a new colour. Allow the completed designs to dry for at least 24 hours.

10. Once the paint is completely dry, scratch off any paint that may have got on the copper foil.

11. Using a small paintbrush, apply the transparent frost texture, smoothly and evenly, to the **painted** areas. Frosting takes from one to 10 hours to dry, depending on the temperature, and will prevent the paintwork from getting scratched.

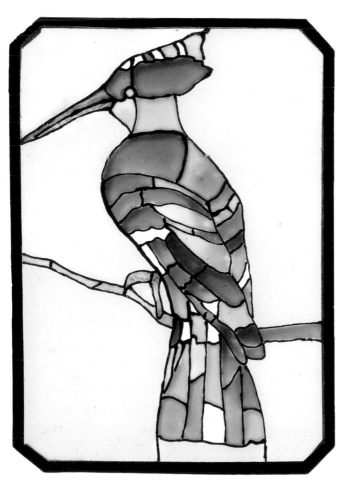

NOTE: *Transparent frost texture is ideal for creating different effects, such as stippling and marbling. Once dry, the frost texture is as clear as glass. Experiment on a piece of scrap glass and you will be surprised at what can be achieved.*

12. Once the frost texture has dried, thin down the yacht varnish with a little bit of turpentine thinners and carefully apply a coat to the painted areas. Allow to dry for 24 hours. If you have accidentally got varnish on the copper foil, scratch it off with your craft knife.

13. Make small loops from copper wire and attach one with a spot of solder to the top centre of each piece of glass. Brush the copper foil with flux and flow solder round the edge of each piece of glass.

14. Using a soft rag, rub grey patina over the soldered areas so that they blend in with the leaded areas.

15. Use thin wooden dowels or metal rods and fine fishing line and assemble the mobile in the usual way.

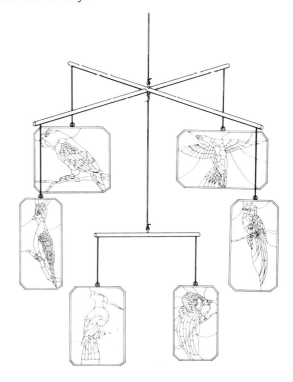

CANDLE LIGHT-CATCHERS

Brighten up a dinner party table setting with these attractive candle-holders. The templates for the abstract design can be found on page 84 and for the flower design on page 83.

1. If necessary, enlarge the templates onto graph paper and ask your glass merchant to cut pieces of glass to measure. Remember to have the corner stabilizing pieces cut as well. Gently sandstone the edges of the glass as described on page 6.

NOTE: *Remember to use a rag to hold and move the glass so as not to cut your hands. Once all the edges have been lightly rubbed, the glass will be safe to handle.*

2. Wash the pieces of glass with the ammoniac-based cleaning detergent, then dry them thoroughly with kitchen paper towel.

3. Surround each piece of glass (including the triangular stabilizers) with 10 mm to 12 mm (3⁄8 in to 1⁄2 in) wide copper foil as follows: Remove a small piece of the thin paper backing on the copper foil and, beginning at one corner, centre the copper foil along one edge of the glass. Slowly stick the copper foil all the way round the edge until you reach the beginning, then overlap by 6 mm (1⁄4 in). (If you find the copper foil is not going on straight, pull it off and adjust it.) Using a piece of smooth wood, press along the entire length of the copper foil, then fold the edges over with your fingers. Press firmly to ensure that the foil sticks to the glass and then, using the piece of smooth wood, press along the entire length of both edges.

4. Using a black felt-tip pen, trace the design of your choice onto a sheet of paper and colour it in with pencil crayons.

5. Tape the design template to your work surface, which should be covered with a blanket, and position the prepared glass on top. Use a piece of Prestik (Blu-Tack) on each corner to hold it in place.

6. Follow the lines of the design with the adhesive lead (pull it off and adjust it if you are not following the lines accurately), overlapping pieces where necessary (see *Using adhesive lead* on page 7).

7. Turn each piece of glass over and, following the lines of the adhesive lead, squeeze on the liquid lead. Apply even pressure and start at the top left-hand corner and work across and then down, so that there is no danger of smudging the wet liquid lead with your arm or hand. Wipe the nozzle of the tube or bottle on a rag before beginning each new line. Allow to dry for at least two hours.

NOTE: *If you make a mistake, complete the liquid leading and allow it to dry. After about two hours, scrape off the offending line or smudge with your craft knife. Reapply the liquid lead and again allow it to dry thoroughly.*

8. Once the liquid lead is completely dry, wipe off any fingermarks on the glass with a soft rag and window cleaner.

9. Follow the instructions on using glass paints on page 7 and once you are happy with the shade and texture of each colour, begin painting, using the darkest colours first. Once again, begin at the top of the design and work downward, remembering to allow each area to dry before painting an adjacent area. This is very important as the colour in one area may overflow and mix with the colour next to it. Clean your paintbrush thoroughly with thinners before using a new colour. Allow the completed design to dry for at least 24 hours.

10. Once the paint has dried completely, use your craft knife to scratch off any paint that may have got onto the copper foil.

11. Using a 4 cm (1½ in) or 5 cm (2 in) wide paintbrush, apply the transparent frost texture, smoothly and evenly, to the **painted** areas. Frosting takes from one to 10 hours to dry, depending on the temperature, and will prevent the paintwork from getting scratched.

NOTE: *Transparent frost texture is ideal for creating different effects, such as stippling and marbling. Once dry, the frost texture is as clear as glass. Experiment on a piece of scrap glass and you will be surprised at what can be achieved.*

12. Once the frost texture has dried, thin down the yacht varnish with a little bit of turpentine thinners and carefully apply a coat to the painted areas. Allow to dry for 24 hours. If you have accidentally got varnish on the copper foil, scratch it off with your craft knife.

13. Lay the four sides of the candle light-catcher, painted side up, on your work surface and tape them together with masking tape. Remember to leave a 2 mm (¹⁄₁₆ in) gap between each piece of glass. Carefully lift the taped pieces and tape the remaining opening sides together. Brush the corners with flux and spot solder all the joints.

14. When you are satisfied with the fit, remove the tape, brush flux along the copper-foiled edges and flow solder (see page 9) until the candle light-catcher is completely soldered on the outside.

15. Brush flux along the inner seams of the candle light-catcher and flow solder carefully so as not to get solder on the paint.

16. Turn the candle light-catcher over and brush flux on the inner corners. Spot solder the triangular stabilizers in position.

17. Solder round the top edge of the candle light-catcher as well, then using a soft cloth, rub a little grey patina onto the silvery soldered areas so that they blend in with the adhesive lead.

18. To use, light a 7 cm (2¾ in) or 8 cm (3 in) diameter candle and lower the candle light-catcher over it. Be sure to position the candle in the centre.

LAMPSHADES

Make these beautiful lamps and paint them to coordinate with the decor of your room. The templates can be found on pages 85-89.

THE METHOD

1. Enlarge the templates onto graph paper and ask your glass merchant to cut pieces of glass to measure. You will need six pieces of glass cut from each template. Gently sandstone the edges as described on page 6.

NOTE: *Remember to use a rag to hold and move the glass so as not to cut your hands. Once all the edges have been lightly rubbed, the glass will be safe to handle.*

2. Wash the pieces of glass with the ammoniac-based cleaning detergent, then dry them thoroughly with kitchen paper towel.

3. Surround each piece of glass with 10 mm to 12 mm (3⁄8 in to 1⁄2 in) wide copper foil as follows: Remove a small piece of the thin paper backing on the copper foil and, beginning at one corner, centre the copper foil along one edge of the glass. Slowly stick the copper foil all the way round the edge until you reach the beginning, then overlap by 6 mm (1⁄4 in). (If you find the copper foil is not going on straight, pull it off and adjust it.) Using a piece of smooth wood, press along the entire length of the copper foil, then fold the edges over with your fingers. Press firmly to ensure that the foil sticks to the glass and then, using the piece of smooth wood, press along the entire length of both edges.

4. Make a tracing of the design template on a piece of paper and cut it out. (*For the parrot lamp only*, make tracings of each template on sheets of paper and cut them out. Arrange the templates as shown opposite, sticking them together with masking tape.) If you have not decided on a colour scheme, colour in the design using pencil crayons.

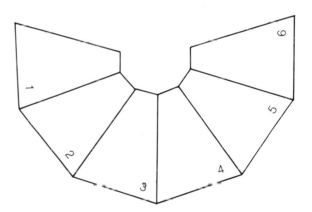

5. Tape the templates to your work surface, which should be covered with a blanket, and position the prepared glass on top. Use pieces of Prestik (Blu-Tack) to hold them in place.

6. Now follow the lines of the design with the adhesive lead (pull it off and adjust it if you are not following the lines accurately), overlapping pieces where necessary (see *Using adhesive lead* on page 7).

7. Turn each piece of glass over and, following the lines of the adhesive lead, squeeze on the liquid lead. Apply even pressure and start at the top left-hand corner and work across and then down, so that there is no danger of smudging the wet liquid lead with your arm or hand. Wipe the nozzle of the tube or bottle on a rag before beginning each new line. Allow to dry for at least two hours.

NOTE: *If you make a mistake, complete the liquid leading and allow it to dry. After about two hours, scrape off the offending line or smudge with your lead or craft knife. Reapply the liquid lead and again allow it to dry thoroughly.*

8. Once the liquid lead is completely dry, wipe off any fingermarks on the glass with a soft rag and window cleaner.

9. Follow the instructions on using glass paints on page 7 and once you are happy with the shade and texture of each colour, begin painting, using the darkest colours first. Once again, begin at the top of the design and work downward, remembering to allow each area to dry before painting an adjacent area. This is very important as the colour in one area may overflow and mix with the colour next to it. Clean your paintbrush thoroughly with thinners before using a new colour. Allow the completed design to dry for at least 24 hours.

10. Once the paint has dried completely, use your lead or craft knife to scratch off any paint that may have got onto the copper foil.

11. Using a 4 cm (1½ in) or 5 cm (2 in) wide paintbrush, apply the transparent frost texture, smoothly and evenly, to the **painted** areas. Frosting takes from one to 10 hours to dry, depending on the temperature, and will prevent the paintwork from getting scratched.

NOTE: *Transparent frost texture is ideal for creating different effects, such as stippling and marbling. Once dry, the frost texture is as clear as glass. Experiment on a piece of scrap glass and you will be surprised at what can be achieved.*

12. Once the frost texture has dried, thin down the yacht varnish with a little bit of turpentine thinners and carefully apply a coat to the painted areas. Allow to dry for 24 hours. If you have accidentally got varnish on the copper foil, scratch it off with your craft knife.

13. Lay the twelve sections (six sections for the *parrot* lamp), painted side up, on your work surface and tape the sections together with masking tape, leaving a 2 mm (1/16 in) gap between each piece of glass (see illustration below). Carefully lift the taped panels to form a conical shape and tape the remaining open sides together. Brush with flux and spot solder top and bottom as shown.

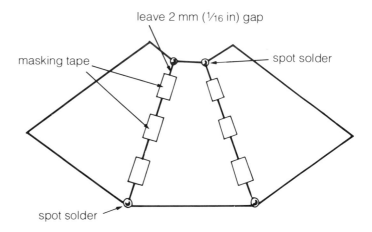

NOTE: *You may want to crumple up pieces of newspaper and place them in a cardboard box and then rest the lamp on the newspaper before fluxing and soldering.*

14. When you are happy with the fit, brush on flux and flow solder along the seams, first on the outside, then on the inside of the lamp.

15. Using an iron ring and 2 mm to 3 mm (1/16 in to 1/8 in) thick wire, solder the wire to the ring to make a six-legged spider that will fit the top of the lamp. Bend the legs as shown in the illustration below.

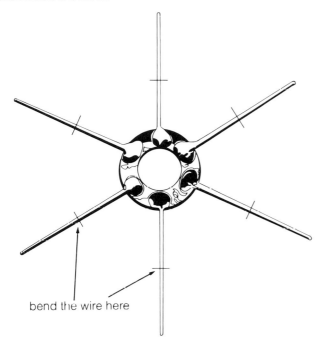

bend the wire here

16. Clean the spider by sanding it with fine metal sandpaper. Turn the lamp upside down, brush with flux and, centring the spider in the opening, spot solder the spider to the seams of the lamp. When you are satisfied with the fit, brush sparingly with flux and flow solder.

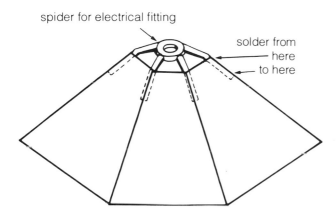

spider for electrical fitting

solder from here to here

17. To make the top section, tape together the twelve pieces of glass cut from templates C and D (for the *parrot* lamp, the six pieces cut from template H), remembering to leave a 2 mm (1/16 in) gap between each piece.

18. Brush the joints with flux and spot solder. Remove the tape, brush the seams with flux and flow solder along the outer and inner seams.

19. Now tape the top section to the main section of the lamp, remembering to leave a 2 mm (1/16 in) gap between each piece. Brush with flux and spot solder.

20. Remove the tape, brush the inner and outer seams with flux and flow solder.

21. Tape the remaining pieces of glass together to form the bottom of the lamp, again remembering to leave a 2 mm (1/16 in) gap between each piece of glass. Brush with flux and spot solder.

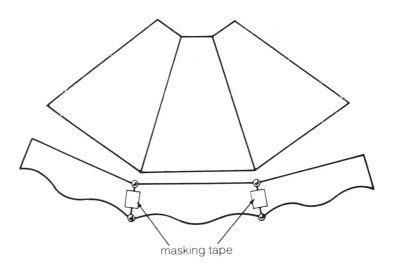

masking tape

22. Remove the tape, brush with flux and flow solder along the outer and inner seams.

23. Now tape this bottom section to the main section of the lamp, again remembering to leave a 2 mm (1/16 in) gap between each piece. Brush with flux and spot solder.

24. Remove the tape, brush flux along the seams and flow solder carefully along the outer and inner seams.

25. Using a soft cloth, rub grey patina on the silvery soldered areas so that they blend in with the grey of the adhesive lead.

26. Take the lamp to an electrical shop and have a light bulb socket and flex fitted as well as a chain to hang the lamp.

NOTE: *These designs can also be used to make standing lamps. If you are working with the parrot design, however, omit the top section (that is, the pieces of glass cut from template H), as the parrot standing lamp looks better without it. Measure the diameter of the bottom opening of each lamp and make a six-legged spider to fit. Attach the spider as described in Steps 15 and 16.*

VASE

This pretty vase makes an ideal gift for a special friend. The templates for this design can be found on page 90.

The templates for this design can be found on page 90.

THE METHOD

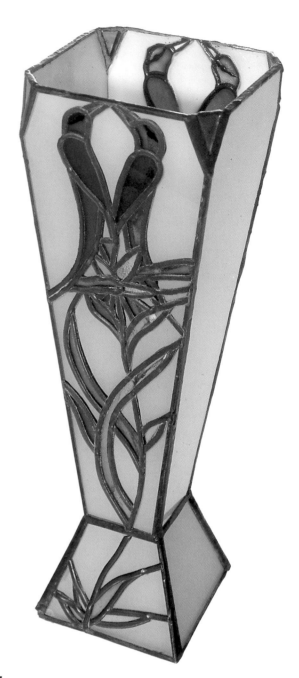

1. Enlarge the templates onto graph paper and ask your glass merchant to cut pieces of glass to measure. You will need four pieces of glass cut from each of templates A, B and C and one from template D. Gently sandstone the edges as described on page 6.

NOTE: *Remember to use a rag to hold and move the glass so as not to cut your hands. Once all the edges have been lightly rubbed, the glass will be safe to handle.*

2. Wash the pieces of glass with the ammoniac-based cleaning detergent, then dry them thoroughly with kitchen paper towel.

3. Surround each piece of glass with 10 mm to 12 mm (⅜ in to ½ in) wide copper foil as follows: Remove a small piece of the thin paper backing on the copper foil and, beginning at one corner, centre the copper foil along one edge of the glass. Slowly stick the copper foil all the way round the edge until you reach the beginning, then overlap by 6 mm (¼ in). (If you find the copper foil is not going on straight, pull it off and adjust it.) Using a piece of smooth wood, press along the entire length of the copper foil, then fold the edges over with your fingers. Press firmly to ensure that the foil sticks to the glass and then, using the piece of smooth wood, press along the entire length of both edges.

4. Make a tracing of the design on templates A and B. If you have not decided on a colour scheme, colour in the design using pencil crayons which can be erased if you are not happy with the end result.

5. Tape the design templates to your work surface, which should be covered with a blanket, and, working only with two of the pieces of glass cut from template A and two cut from template B, position the prepared pieces of glass in turn on top of the design. Use a piece of Prestik (Blu-Tack) on each corner to hold them in place.

6. Now follow the lines of the design with the adhesive lead (pull it off and adjust it if you are not following the lines accurately), overlapping pieces where necessary (see page 7).

7. Turn each piece of glass over and, following the lines of the adhesive lead, squeeze on the liquid lead. Apply even pressure and start at the top left-hand corner and work across and then down, so that there is no danger of smudging the wet liquid lead with your arm or hand. Wipe the nozzle of the tube or bottle on a rag before beginning each new line. Allow to dry for at least two hours.

NOTE: *If you make a mistake, complete the liquid leading and allow it to dry. After about two hours, scrape off the offending line or smudge with your lead or craft knife. Reapply the liquid lead and again allow it to dry thoroughly.*

8. Once the liquid lead is dry, wipe off any fingermarks with a soft rag and window cleaner.

9. Follow the instructions on using glass paints on page 7 and once you are happy with the shade and texture of each colour, begin painting, using the darkest colours first. Once again, begin at the top of the design and work downward, remembering to allow each area to dry before painting an adjacent area. This is very important as the colour in one area may overflow and mix with the colour next to it. Clean your paintbrush thoroughly with thinners before using a new colour. Allow the completed design to dry for at least 24 hours.

10. Using white opaque paint or the colour of your choice, paint the remaining pieces of glass cut from templates A, B and D. Paint the small triangular pieces cut from template C, in the colour of your choice.

11. Once the paint has dried completely, use your craft knife to scratch off any paint that may have got onto the copper foil.

12. Using a 4 cm (1½ in) or 5 cm (2 in) wide paintbrush, apply the transparent frost texture, smoothly and evenly, to the **painted** areas and allow to dry thoroughly.

NOTE: *Transparent frost texture is ideal for creating different effects, such as stippling and marbling. Once dry, the frost texture is as clear as glass. Experiment on a piece of scrap glass and you will be surprised at what can be achieved.*

13. Once the frost texture has dried, thin down the yacht varnish with a little bit of turpentine thinners and carefully apply a coat to the painted areas. Allow to dry for 24 hours. If you have accidentally got varnish on the copper foil, scratch it off with your craft knife.

14. Use masking tape to tape together the four sections cut from template A, leaving a 2 mm (1/16 in) gap between each piece of glass. Brush with flux and spot solder top and bottom.

15. When you are happy with the fit, brush on flux and flow solder along the seams, first on the outside, then on the inside.

16. Tape together the four sections cut from template B, brush with flux and spot solder. Check the fit with the top of the vase, then flow solder along the outer and inner seams.

17. Tape the bottom of the vase (cut from template D) to the base, brush with flux and spot solder. Remove the tape and flow solder along the outer and inner seams.

18. Tape the four corner pieces in position, brush with flux and spot solder. Remove the tape, brush with flux and flow solder along the outer and inner seams.

19. Using a small brush, apply yacht varnish to all the inner seams to make them water-tight.

20. Using a soft cloth, rub grey patina onto the silvery soldered areas on the outside of the vase so that they blend in with the adhesive lead.

FRUIT BOWLS

Two beautiful bowls in which to display fresh fruit. Templates for the blue fruit bowl can be found on page 92 and for the orange one on page 91.

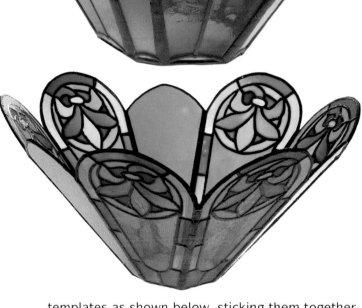

THE METHOD

1. Enlarge the templates for the fruit bowl of your choice onto graph paper and ask your glass merchant to cut pieces of glass to measure. *For the blue fruit bowl, you will need six pieces of glass cut from template A, three cut from template B and one from template C. For the orange fruit bowl, you will need five pieces cut from template A, five from template B and one from template C.* Gently sandstone the edges as described on page 6.

NOTE: *Remember to use a rag to hold and move the glass so as not to cut your hands. Once all the edges have been lightly rubbed, the glass will be safe to handle.*

2. Wash the pieces of glass with the ammoniac-based cleaning detergent, then dry them thoroughly with kitchen paper towel.

3. Surround each piece of glass with 10 mm to 12 mm (3⁄8 in to 1⁄2 in) wide copper foil as follows: Remove a small piece of the thin paper backing on the copper foil and, beginning at one corner, centre the copper foil along one edge of the glass. Slowly stick the copper foil all the way round the edge until you reach the beginning, then overlap by 6 mm (1⁄4 in). (If you find the copper foil is not going on straight, pull it off and adjust it.) Using a piece of smooth wood, press along the entire length of the copper foil, then fold the edges over with your fingers. Press firmly to ensure that the foil sticks to the glass and then, using the piece of smooth wood, press along the entire length of both edges.

4. Make tracings of templates A and B on sheets of paper and cut them out. Arrange the templates as shown below, sticking them together with masking tape. If you have not decided on a colour scheme, colour in the design using pencil crayons which can be erased if you are not happy with the results.

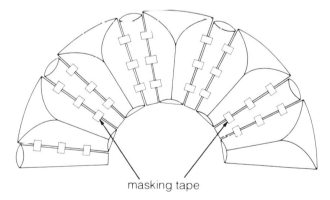

masking tape

5. Tape template A (for the blue fruit bowl) or templates A and B (for the orange fruit bowl) to your work surface, which should be covered with a blanket, and position the prepared glass on top. Use pieces of Prestik (Blu-Tack) to hold the glass in place.

6. Now follow the lines of the design with the adhesive lead (pull it off and adjust it if you are not following the lines accurately), overlapping pieces where necessary (see page 7). Repeat with the remaining pieces of glass.

7. Turn each piece of glass over and, following the lines of the adhesive lead, squeeze on the liquid lead. Apply even pressure and start at the top left-hand corner and work across and then down, so that there is no danger of smudging the wet liquid lead with your arm or hand. Wipe the nozzle of the tube or bottle on a rag before beginning each new line. Allow to dry for at least two hours.

NOTE: *If you make a mistake, complete the liquid leading and allow it to dry. After about two hours, scrape off the offending line or smudge with your lead or craft knife. Reapply the liquid lead and again allow it to dry thoroughly.*

8. Once the liquid lead is completely dry, wipe off any fingermarks on the glass with a soft rag and window cleaner.

9. Follow the instructions on using glass paints on page 7 and paint the pieces of glass corresponding to template A, using the darkest colours first. Begin at the top of the design and work downward, remembering to allow each area to dry before painting an adjacent area as the colour in one area may overflow and mix with the colour next to it. Clean your paintbrush thoroughly with thinners before using a new colour. Now paint the pieces corresponding to templates B and C. Allow the completed design to dry for 24 hours.

10. Once the paint has dried completely, use your lead or craft knife to scratch off any paint that may have got onto the copper foil.

11. Using a 4 cm (1½ in) or 5 cm (2 in) wide paintbrush, apply the transparent frost texture, smoothly and evenly, to the **painted** areas. Frosting takes from one to 10 hours to dry, depending on the temperature, and will prevent the paintwork from getting scratched.

NOTE: *Transparent frost texture is ideal for creating different effects, such as stippling and marbling. Once dry, the frost texture is as clear as glass. Experiment on a piece of scrap glass and you will be surprised at what can be achieved.*

12. Once the frost texture has dried, thin down the yacht varnish with a little bit of turpentine thinners and carefully apply a coat to the painted areas. Allow to dry for 24 hours. If you have accidentally got varnish on the copper foil, scratch it off with your craft knife.

13. Lay the sections, painted side up, on your work surface and tape the sections together with masking tape, leaving a 2 mm (1/16 in) gap between each piece of glass (see illustration below). Carefully lift the taped panels to form a conical shape and tape the remaining open sides together. Brush with flux and spot solder top and bottom as shown.

leave 2 mm (1/16 in) gap

spot solder

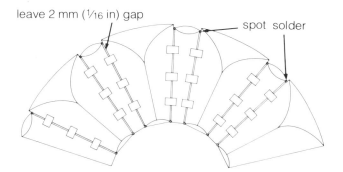

14. When you are happy with the fit, remove the tape, brush on flux and flow solder along the seams, first on the outside, then on the inside.

15. Turn the bowl upside down (you may want to crumple up pieces of newspaper and place them in a cardboard box and then rest the bowl on the newspaper) and tape the piece of glass cut from template C in position. Brush the copper foil with flux and spot solder. Remove the tape, brush with flux and flow solder along the seams, both outside and inside the bowl.

16. Using a soft cloth, rub grey patina on the silvery soldered areas so that they blend in with the grey of the adhesive lead.

POT-PLANT HOLDER

Brighten up your plants with a stained glass pot-plant holder. The templates can be found on page 93.

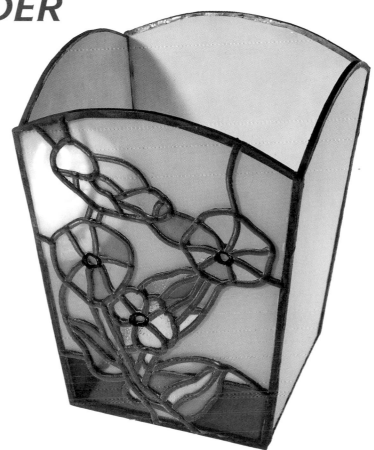

THE METHOD

1. Enlarge the templates for the pot-plant holder onto graph paper and ask your glass merchant to cut pieces of glass the size of the templates. Gently sandstone the edges as described on page 6.

NOTE: *Remember to use a rag to hold and move the glass so as not to cut your hands. Once all the edges have been lightly rubbed, the glass will be safe to handle.*

2. Wash the pieces of glass with the ammoniac-based cleaning detergent, then dry them thoroughly with kitchen paper towel.

3. Surround each piece of glass with 10 mm to 12 mm (3/8 in to 1/2 in) wide copper foil as follows: Remove a small piece of the thin paper backing on the copper foil and, beginning at one corner, centre the copper foil along one edge of the glass. Slowly stick the copper foil all the way round the edge until you reach the beginning, then overlap by 6 mm (1/4 in). Using a piece of smooth wood, press along the entire length of the copper foil, then fold the edges over with your fingers. Press firmly to ensure that the foil sticks to the glass and then, using the piece of smooth wood, press along the entire length of both edges.

4. Make a tracing of the design on a sheet of paper and, if you have not decided on a colour scheme, colour it in using pencil crayons which can be erased if you are not happy with the results.

5. Tape the design template to your work surface, which should be covered with a blanket, and position the prepared glass on top. Use pieces of Prestik (Blu-Tack) to hold the glass in place.

6. Now follow the lines of the design with the adhesive lead (pull it off and adjust it if you are not following the lines accurately), overlapping pieces where necessary (see *Using adhesive lead* on page 7).

7. Turn the piece of glass over and, following the lines of the adhesive lead, squeeze on the liquid lead. Apply even pressure and start at the top left-hand corner and work across and then down, so that there is no danger of smudging the wet liquid lead with your arm or hand. Wipe the nozzle of the tube or bottle on a rag before beginning each new line. Allow to dry for at least two hours.

NOTE: *If you make a mistake, complete the liquid leading and allow it to dry. After about two hours, scrape off the offending line or smudge with your lead or craft knife. Reapply the liquid lead and again allow it to dry thoroughly.*

8. Once the liquid lead is completely dry, wipe off any fingermarks on the glass with a soft rag and window cleaner.

9. Follow the instructions on using glass paints on page 7 and once you are happy with the shade and texture of each colour, paint the design, using the darkest colours first. Once again, begin at the top of the design and work downward, remembering to allow each area to dry before painting an adjacent area. This is very important as the colour in one area may overflow and mix with the colour next to it. Clean your paintbrush thoroughly with thinners before using a new colour. Allow the completed design to dry for at least 24 hours. Now paint the remaining three sides and the base of the pot-plant holder, using white or a colour of your choice.

10. Once the paint has dried completely (this will take about 24 hours), use your lead or craft knife to scratch off any paint that may have got onto the copper foil.

11. Using a 4 cm (1½ in) or 5 cm (2 in) wide paintbrush, apply the transparent frost texture, smoothly and evenly, to the **painted** areas. Frosting takes from one to 10 hours to dry, depending on the temperature, and will prevent the paintwork from getting scratched.

12. Once the frost texture has dried, thin down the yacht varnish with a little bit of turpentine thinners and carefully apply a coat to the painted areas. Allow to dry for 24 hours. If you have accidentally got varnish on the copper foil, scratch it off with your craft knife.

13. Tape the four sections of the pot-plant holder together with masking tape, leaving a 2 mm (1/16 in) gap between each piece of glass. Brush the copper foil with flux and spot solder the pieces together.

14. When you are happy with the fit, remove the tape, brush on flux and flow solder along the seams, first on the outside, then on the inside.

15. Turn the pot-plant holder upside down (you may want to crumple up pieces of newspaper and place them in a cardboard box and then rest the pot-plant holder on the newspaper) and tape the base in position. Brush the copper foil with flux and spot solder. Remove the tape, brush with flux and flow solder along the seams, both outside and inside the pot-plant holder.

16. Using a soft cloth, rub grey patina on the silvery soldered areas so that they blend in with the grey of the adhesive lead.

HANGING TERRARIUM

This pretty terrarium makes a delightful gift that will enhance a sunny room. The templates can be found on page 94.

THE METHOD

1. Enlarge the templates to three times the size onto pieces of graph paper and ask your glass merchant to cut four pieces of glass from each of templates A, B, C, D and E and one from template F. Gently sandstone the edges as described on page 6.

NOTE: *Remember to use a rag to hold and move the glass so as not to cut your hands. Once all the edges have been lightly rubbed, the glass will be safe to handle.*

2. Wash the pieces of glass with the ammoniac-based cleaning detergent, then dry them thoroughly with kitchen paper towel.

3. Surround each piece of glass with 10 mm to 12 mm (³⁄8 in to ½ in) wide copper foil as follows: Remove a small piece of the thin paper backing on the copper foil and, beginning at one corner, centre the copper foil along one edge of the glass. Slowly stick the copper foil all the way round the edge until you reach the beginning, then overlap by 6 mm (¼ in). (If you find the copper foil is not going on straight, pull it off and adjust it.) Using a piece of smooth wood, press along the entire length of the copper foil, then fold the edges over with your fingers. Press firmly to ensure that the foil sticks to the glass and then, using the piece of smooth wood, press along the entire length of both edges.

4. Make tracings of the design templates on sheets of paper and, if you have not decided on a colour scheme, colour in the design using pencil crayons which can be erased if you are not happy with the results.

5. Tape the design templates to your work surface, which should be covered with a blanket, and position the prepared glass on top. Use pieces of Prestik (Blu-Tack) to hold the glass in place.

6. Now follow the lines of the design with the adhesive lead (pull it off and adjust it if you are not following the lines accurately), overlapping pieces where necessary (see page 7). Repeat with the remaining pieces of glass.

7. Turn each piece of glass over and, following the lines of the adhesive lead, squeeze on the liquid lead. Apply even pressure and start at the top left-hand corner and work across and then down, so that there is no danger of smudging the wet liquid lead with your arm or hand. Wipe the nozzle of the tube or bottle on a rag before beginning each new line. Allow to dry for at least two hours.

NOTE: *If you make a mistake, complete the liquid leading and allow it to dry. After about two hours, scrape off the offending line or smudge with your lead or craft knife. Reapply the liquid lead and again allow it to dry thoroughly.*

8. Once the liquid lead is completely dry, wipe off any fingermarks on the glass with a soft rag and window cleaner.

9. Follow the instructions on using glass paints on page 7 and once you are happy with the shade and texture of each colour, begin painting, using the darkest colours first. Once again, begin at the top of the design and work downward, remembering to allow each area to dry before painting an adjacent area. This is very important as the colour in one area may overflow and mix with the colour next to it. Clean your paintbrush thoroughly with thinners before using a new colour. Allow the completed design to dry for at least 24 hours.

10. Once the paint has dried completely, use your craft knife to scratch off any paint that may have got onto the copper foil.

11. Using a 4 cm (1½ in) or 5 cm (2 in) wide paintbrush, apply the transparent frost texture, smoothly and evenly, to the **painted** areas. Frosting takes from one to 10 hours to dry, depending on the temperature, and will prevent the paintwork from getting scratched.

NOTE: *Transparent frost texture is ideal for creating different effects, such as stippling and marbling. Once dry, the frost texture is as clear as glass. Experiment on a piece of scrap glass and you will be surprised at what can be achieved.*

12. Once the frost texture has dried, thin down the yacht varnish with a little bit of turpentine thinners and carefully apply a coat to the painted areas. Allow the yacht varnish to dry for at least 24 hours. If you have accidentally got varnish on the copper foil, scratch it off with your craft knife.

13. Tape the four sections of each side together with masking tape, leaving a 2 mm (¹⁄₁₆ in) gap between each piece of glass. Brush the copper foil with flux and spot solder top and bottom as shown.

spot solder

leave 2 mm (¹⁄₁₆ in) gap

14. Now join the four sides together, taping them together with masking tape and remembering to leave a 2 mm (¹⁄₁₆ in) gap between each piece of glass. Brush the copper foil with flux and spot solder top and bottom.

15. When you are happy with the fit, remove the tape, brush the copper foil with flux and flow solder along the outer and inner seams.

16. To make the top of the terrarium, tape the four sides together, leaving a 2 mm (¹⁄₁₆ in) gap between the pieces of glass. Brush the copper foil with flux and spot solder.

17. When you are happy with the fit, remove the tape, brush the copper foil with flux and flow solder along the outer and inner seams.

18. Tape the top section of the terrarium to the base, brush the copper foil with flux and spot solder it in position.

19. Remove the tape, brush the copper foil with flux and flow solder along the outer seams. Turn the terrarium upside down, brush with flux and flow solder along the inner seams.

20. Measure the top of the terrarium and cut a piece of 2 mm (⅛ in) thick wire to fit diagonally across the opening. Add on an extra 5 cm (2 in) either side so that the wire can be soldered onto the inner seams. Make a loop in another piece of wire and cut it to fit the opening, again adding on an extra 5 cm (2 in) on either side.

21. Clean the wire by sanding it with fine metal sandpaper.

22. Push the one piece of wire through the loop of the second piece of wire, brush with flux and spot solder. Now bend the wire 5 cm (2 in) from each end so that it will fit the top opening of the terrarium.

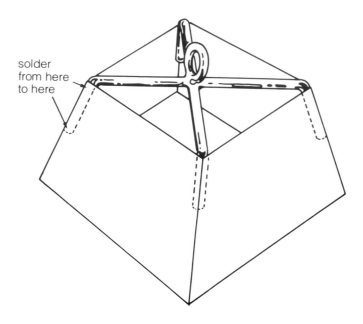

solder from here to here

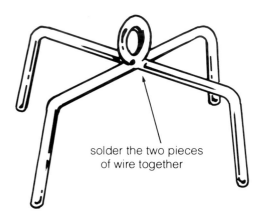

solder the two pieces of wire together

23. Brush with flux and spot solder the wire to the seams as shown. When you are satisfied with the fit, brush with flux and flow solder the wire securely to the seams. Solder the loop securely as well.

24. Turn the terrarium upside down (you may want to crumple up pieces of newspaper and place them in a cardboard box and then rest the terrarium on the newspaper) and tape the base of the terrarium in position. Brush the copper foil with flux and spot solder. Remove the tape, brush with flux and flow solder along the seams, both outside and inside the terrarium.

25. Using a soft cloth, rub grey patina onto the silvery soldered areas so that they blend in with the grey of the adhesive lead.

26. Fill the terrarium with peat moss and add a houseplant of your choice. Attach a chain to the loop and hang up the terrarium.

BELLS

These small bells can be hung singly or in bunches in front of a sunny window. Templates for five different designs can be found on page 95.

THE METHOD

1. Trace the templates onto tracing paper and ask your glass merchant to cut six pieces for the bell and one for the clapper. Gently sandstone the edges as described on page 6.

NOTE: *Remember to use a rag to hold and move the glass so as not to cut your hands. Once all the edges have been lightly rubbed, the glass will be safe to handle.*

2. Wash the pieces of glass with the ammoniac-based cleaning detergent, then dry them thoroughly with kitchen paper towel.

3. Surround each piece of glass with 10 mm to 12 mm (3/8 in to 1/2 in) wide copper foil as follows: Remove a small piece of the thin paper backing on the copper foil and, beginning at one corner, centre the copper foil along one edge of the glass. Slowly stick the copper foil all the way round the edge until you reach the beginning, then overlap by 6 mm (1/4 in). (If you find the copper foil is not going on straight, pull it off and adjust it.) Using a piece of smooth wood, press along the entire length of the copper foil, then fold the edges over with your fingers. Press firmly to ensure that the foil sticks to the glass and then, using the piece of smooth wood, press along the entire length of both edges.

4. Make a tracing of the design template on a sheet of paper and, if you have not decided on a colour scheme, colour in the design using pencil crayons which can be erased if you are not happy with the results.

5. Tape the design template to your work surface, which should be covered with a blanket, and position the prepared glass on top. Use pieces of Prestik (Blu Tack) to hold the glass in place.

6. Now follow the lines of the design with the adhesive lead (pull it off and adjust it if you are not following the lines accurately), overlapping pieces where necessary (see page 7). Repeat with the remaining pieces of glass.

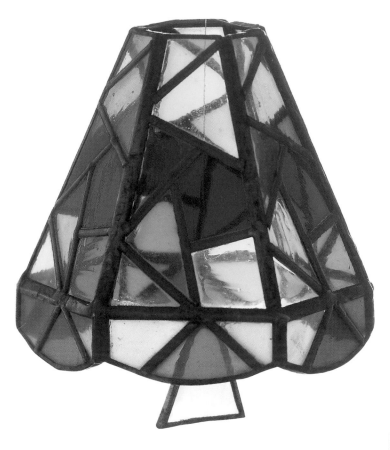

9. Follow the instructions on using glass paints on page 7 and once you are happy with the shade and texture of each colour, begin painting, using the darkest colours first. Once again, begin at the top of the design and work downward, remembering to allow each area to dry before painting an adjacent area. This is very important as the colour in one area may overflow and mix with the colour next to it. Clean your paintbrush thoroughly with thinners before using a new colour. Allow the completed design to dry for at least 24 hours. Remember to paint the clapper.

10. Once the paint has dried completely, use your lead or craft knife to scratch off any paint that may have got onto the copper foil.

11. Using a 4 cm (1½ in) or 5 cm (2 in) wide paintbrush, apply the transparent frost texture, smoothly and evenly, to the **painted** areas. Frosting takes from one to 10 hours to dry, depending on the temperature, and will prevent the paintwork from getting scratched.

NOTE: *Transparent frost texture is ideal for creating different effects, such as stippling and marbling. Once dry, the frost texture is as clear as glass. Experiment on a piece of scrap glass and you will be surprised at what can be achieved.*

12. Once the frost texture has dried, thin down the yacht varnish with a little bit of turpentine thinners and carefully apply a coat to the painted areas. Allow to dry for 24 hours. If you have accidentally got varnish on the copper foil, scratch it off with your craft knife.

13. Lay the six sections of the bell, adhesive lead side down, on your work surface and tape them together with masking tape, leaving a 2 mm (¹⁄₁₆ in) gap between each piece of glass. Carefully lift the taped panels to form a conical shape and tape the remaining open sides together. Brush with flux and spot solder (page 7) top and bottom as shown in the illustration opposite.

7. Turn each piece of glass over and, following the lines of the adhesive lead, squeeze on the liquid lead. Apply even pressure and start at the top left-hand corner and work across and then down, so that there is no danger of smudging the wet liquid lead with your arm or hand. Wipe the nozzle of the tube or bottle on a rag before beginning each new line. Allow to dry for at least two hours.

NOTE: *If you make a mistake, complete the liquid leading and allow it to dry. After about two hours, scrape off the offending line or smudge with your lead or craft knife. Reapply the liquid lead and again allow it to dry thoroughly.*

8. Once the liquid lead is completely dry, wipe off any fingermarks on the glass with a soft rag and window cleaner.

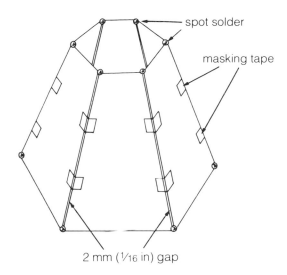

spot solder

masking tape

2 mm (1/16 in) gap

14. When you are happy with the fit, remove the tape, brush the copper foil with flux and flow solder along the outer seams only.

15. Measure the diameter of the top of the bell and add on an extra 3 cm (1 in) to this measurement. Cut a piece of 1 mm (1/32 in) thick wire to this measurement and a second piece of wire slightly longer than this measurement. Make a small loop in the centre of the longer piece of wire. Spot solder the two pieces of wire together and bend the ends as shown.

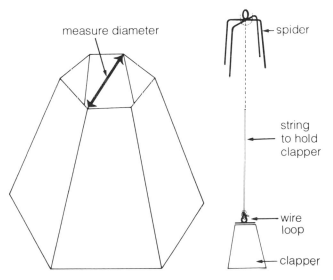

measure diameter

spider

string to hold clapper

wire loop

clapper

16. Brush with flux and solder each end of the wire to opposite seams of the bell as shown in the illustration on page 56.

17. Make a loop from a small piece of 1 mm (1/32 in) thick wire and solder it to the apex of the glass clapper.

18. Thread fine fishing line through the loop in the clapper and tie it to the loop at the top of the bell. Attach a silver chain to the loop at the top of the bell so that it can be hung up.

19. Using a soft cloth, rub grey patina on the silvery soldered areas so that they blend in with the adhesive lead.

Spring morning
Window or door design

Enlarge templates as desired

Sunset
Window or door design

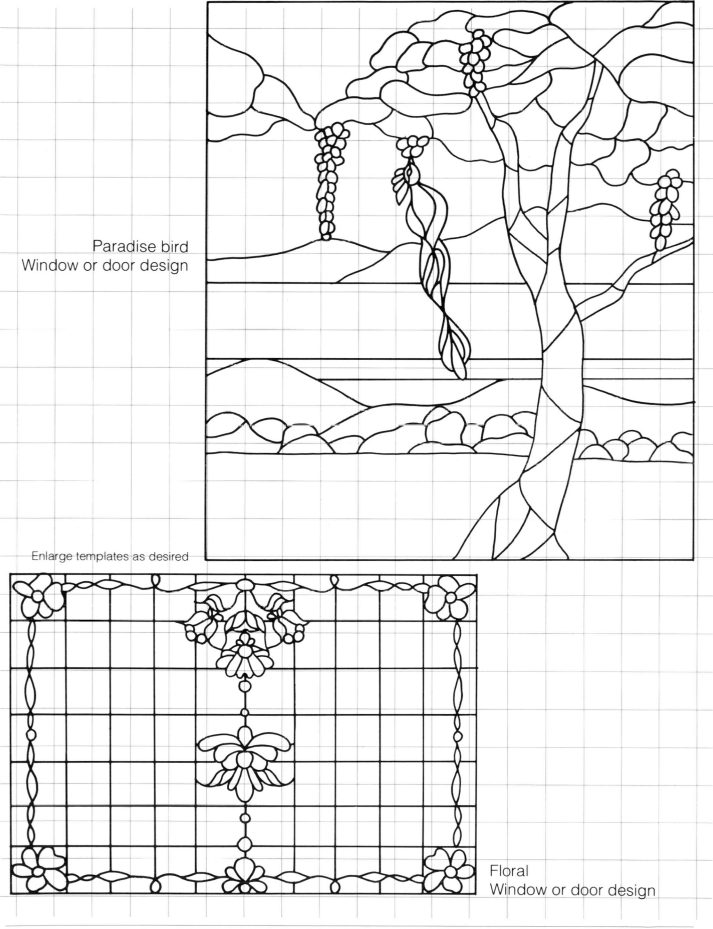

Paradise bird
Window or door design

Enlarge templates as desired

Floral
Window or door design

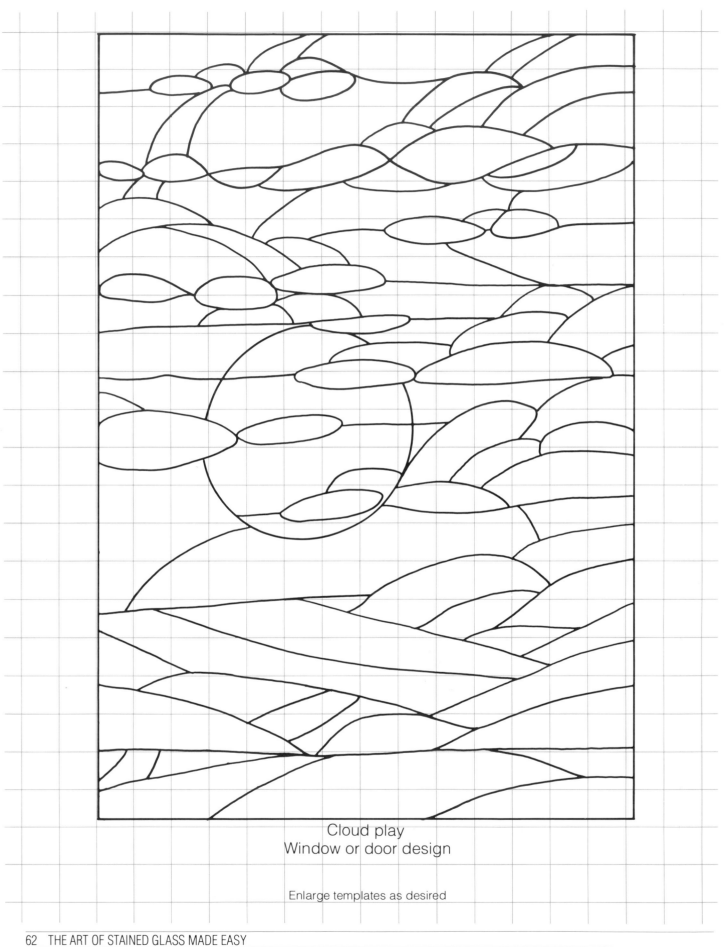

Cloud play
Window or door design

Enlarge templates as desired

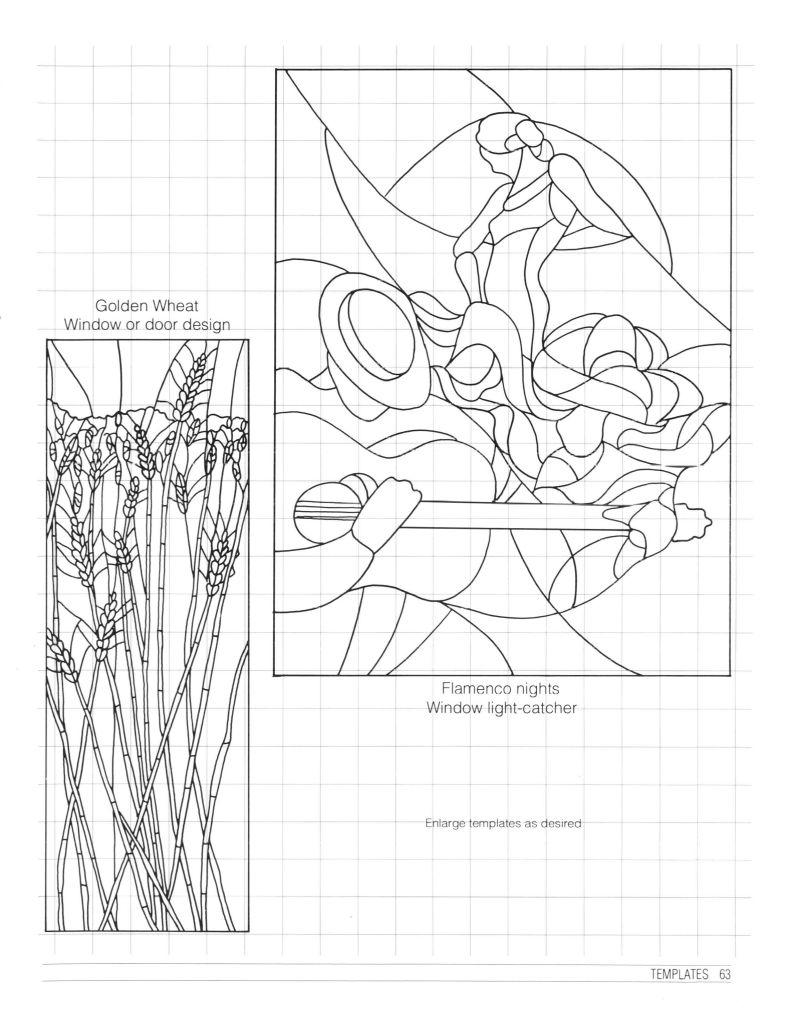

Golden Wheat
Window or door design

Flamenco nights
Window light-catcher

Enlarge templates as desired

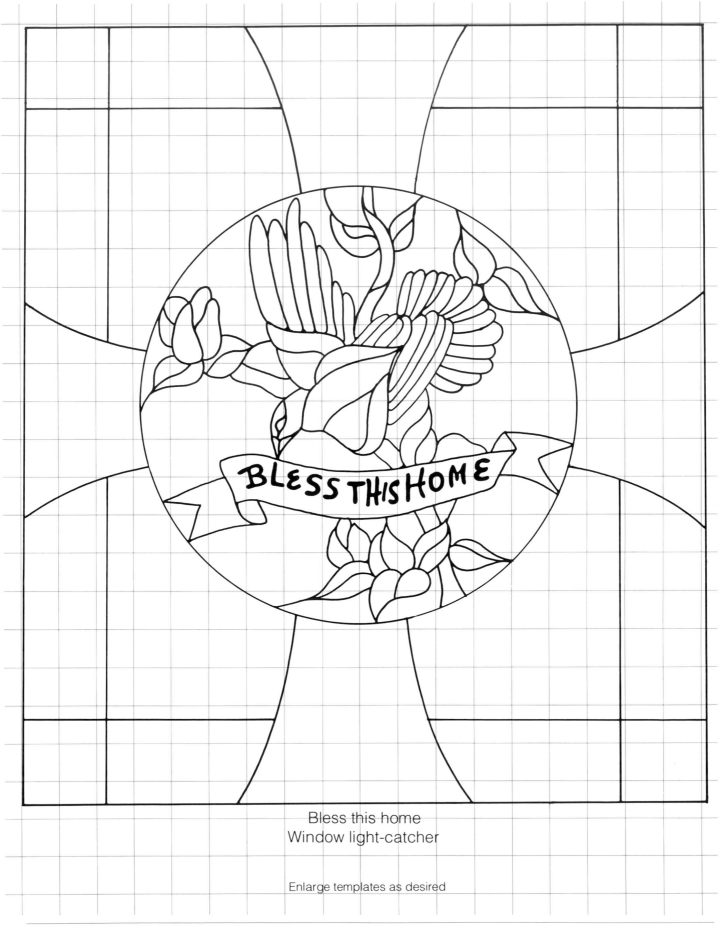

Bless this home
Window light-catcher

Enlarge templates as desired

Chinese garden
Window light-catcher

Enlarge templates as desired

Gondolier
Window light-catcher

My ship
Window light-catcher

Enlarge templates as desired

Side piece (cut 1)

Side piece (cut 1)

Side piece (cut 1)

Side piece (cut 1)

Jewellery box
Model A

Top piece (cut 1)

Enlarge templates by 50%

Base (cut 1)

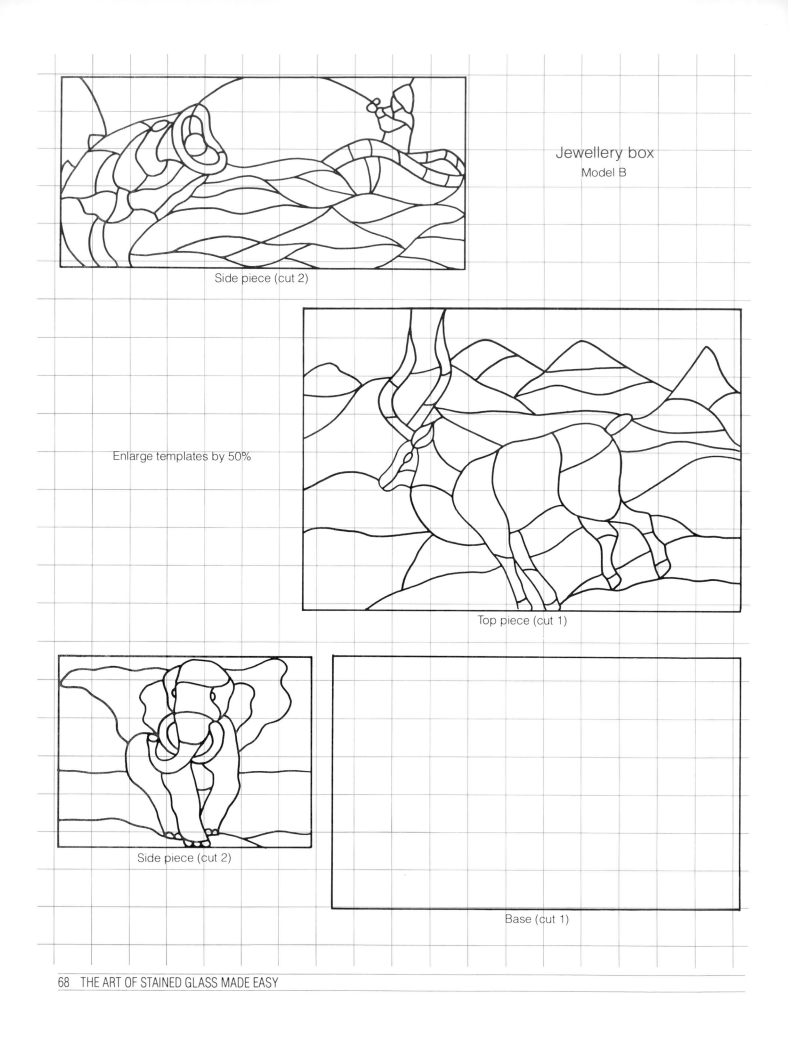

Side piece (cut 2)

Jewellery box
Model B

Enlarge templates by 50%

Top piece (cut 1)

Side piece (cut 2)

Base (cut 1)

Jewellery box
Model C

Top piece (cut 1)

Side piece (cut 2)

Side piece (cut 2)

Enlarge templates by 50%

Base (cut 1)

Wall clock Model A

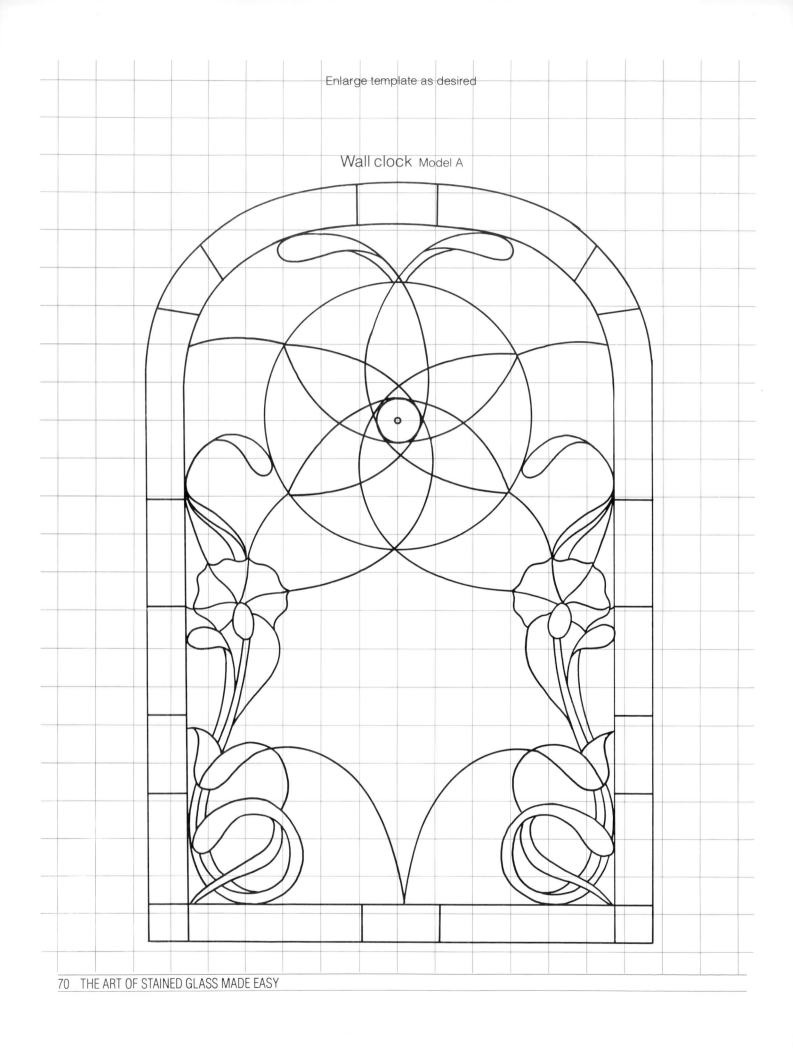

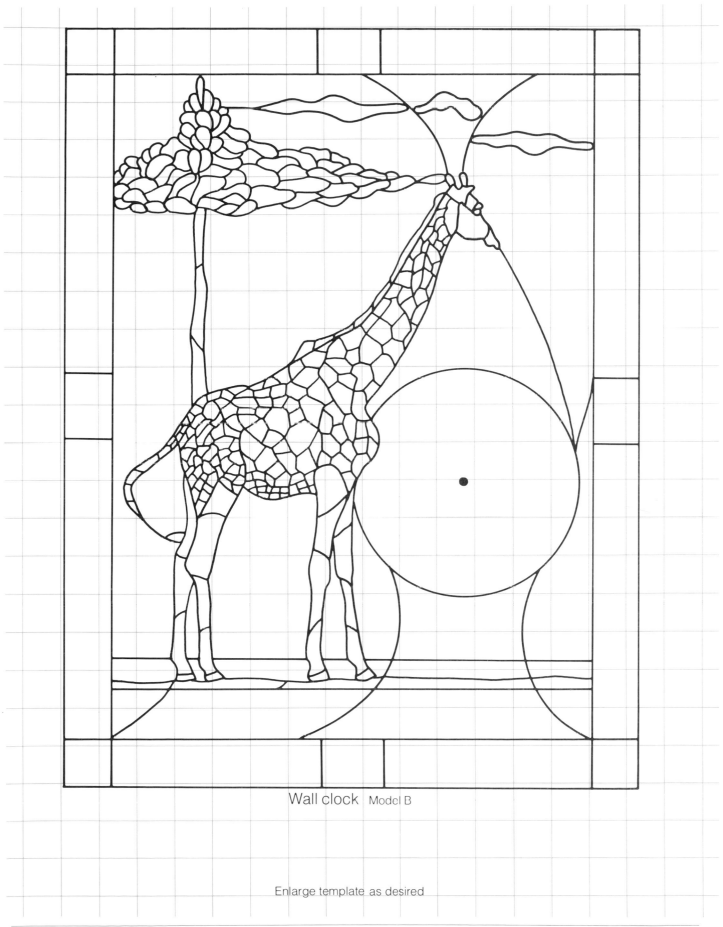

Wall clock | Model B

Enlarge template as desired

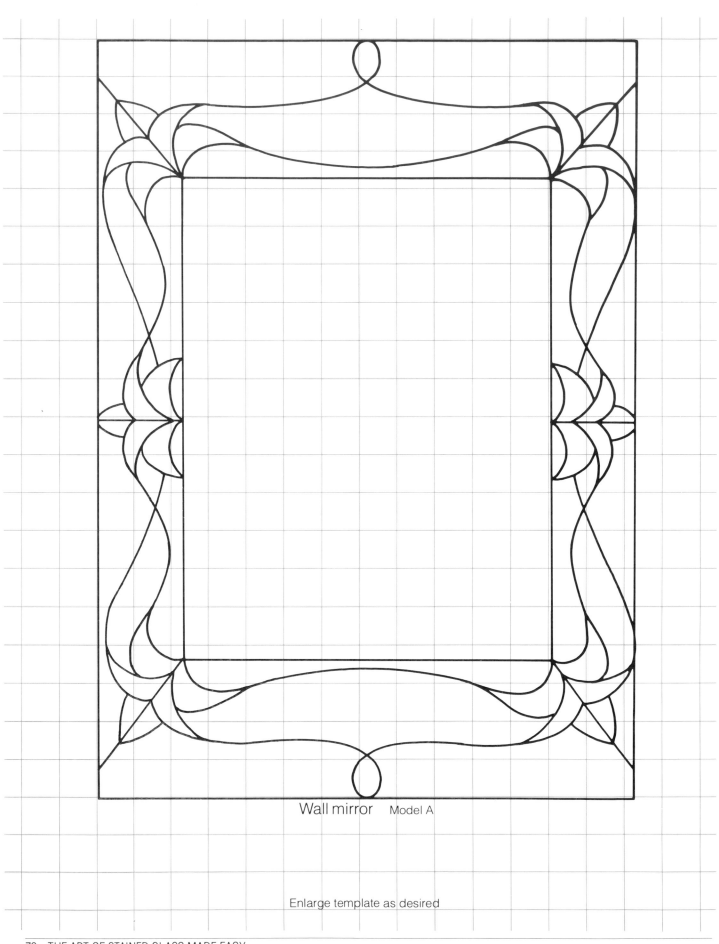

Wall mirror   Model A

Enlarge template as desired

Enlarge template as desired

Wall mirror Model B

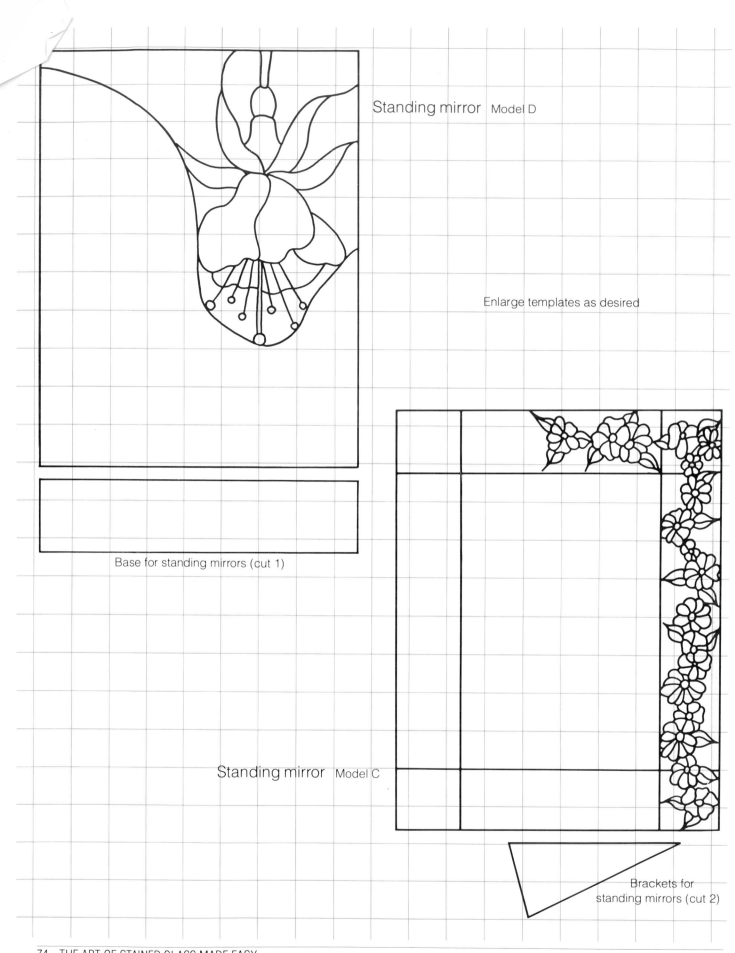

Standing mirror Model D

Enlarge templates as desired

Base for standing mirrors (cut 1)

Standing mirror Model C

Brackets for
standing mirrors (cut 2)

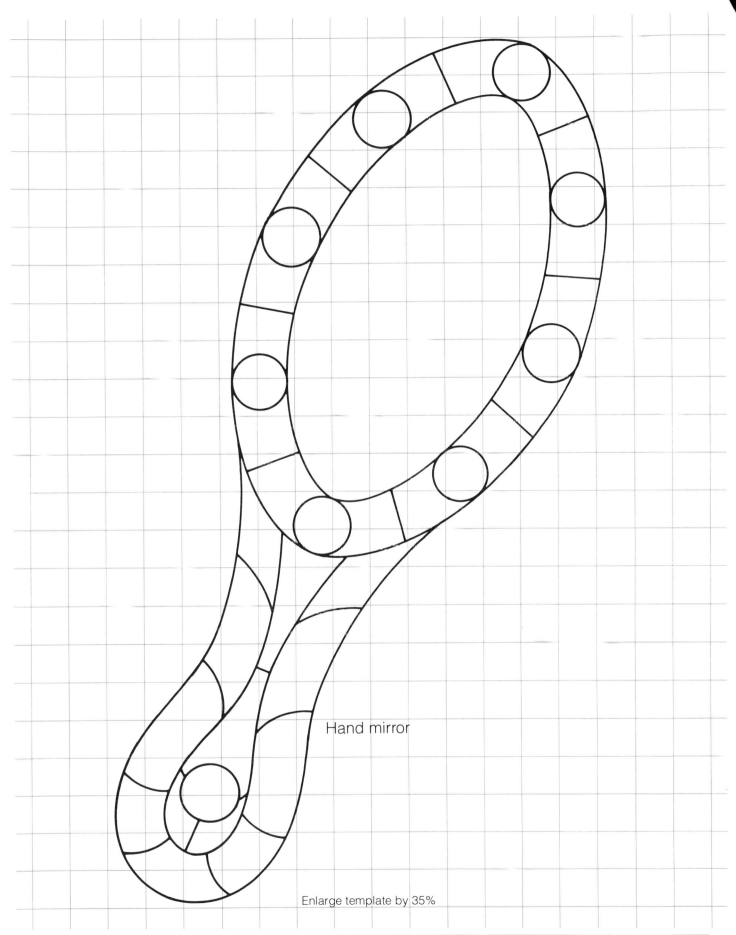

Hand mirror

Enlarge template by 35%

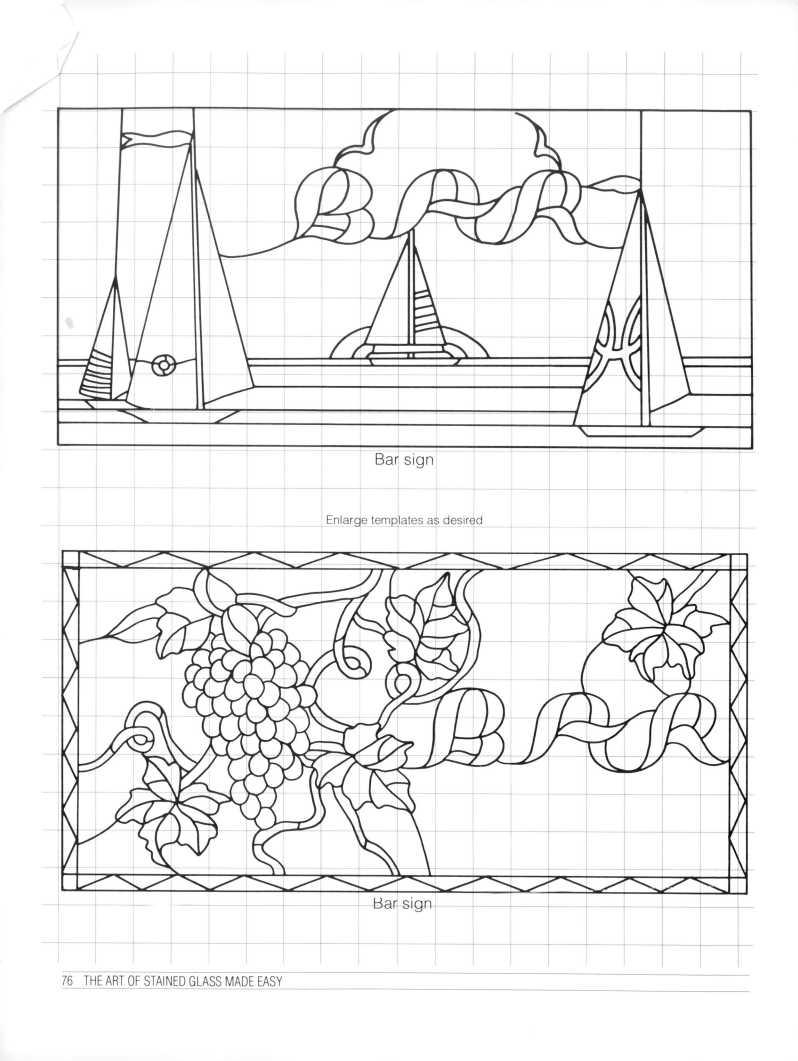

Bar sign

Enlarge templates as desired

Bar sign

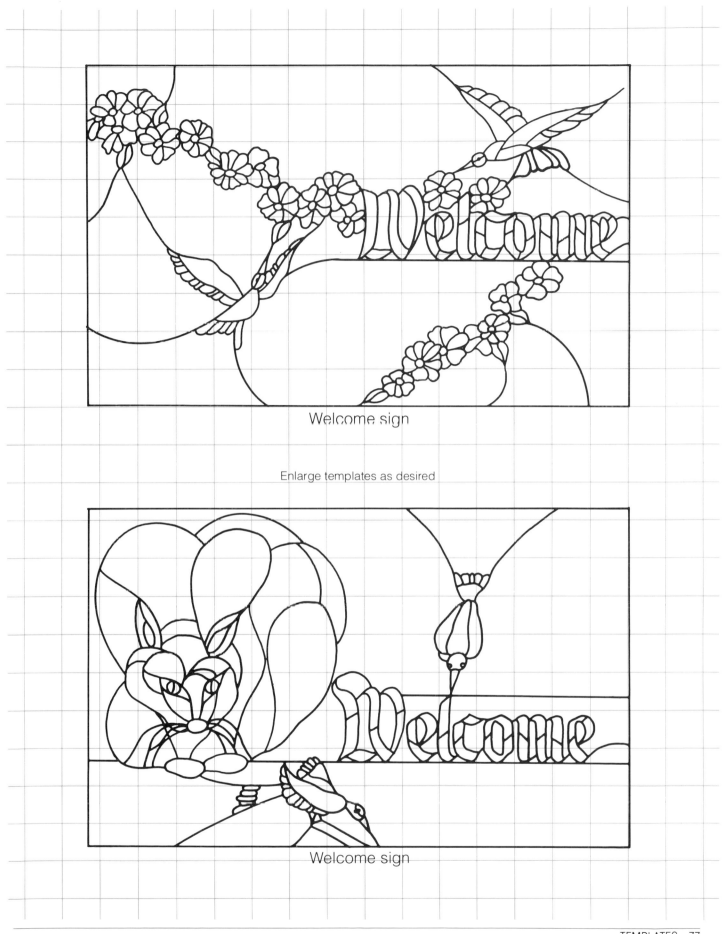

Welcome sign

Enlarge templates as desired

Welcome sign

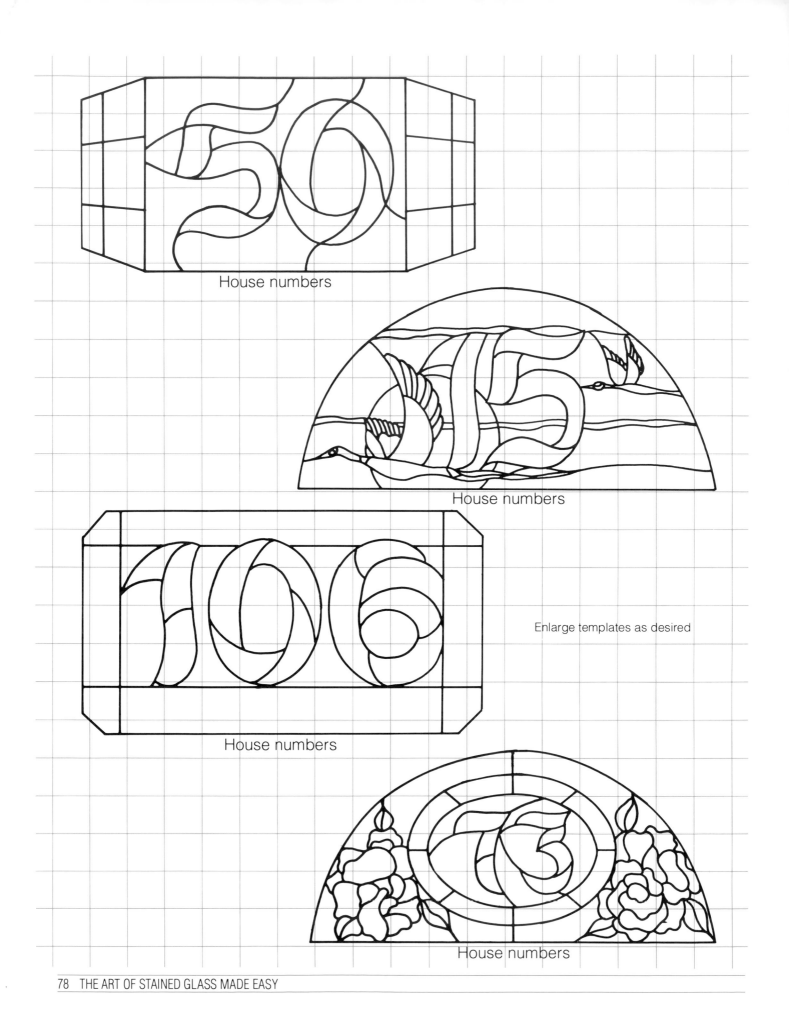

House numbers

House numbers

Enlarge templates as desired

House numbers

House numbers

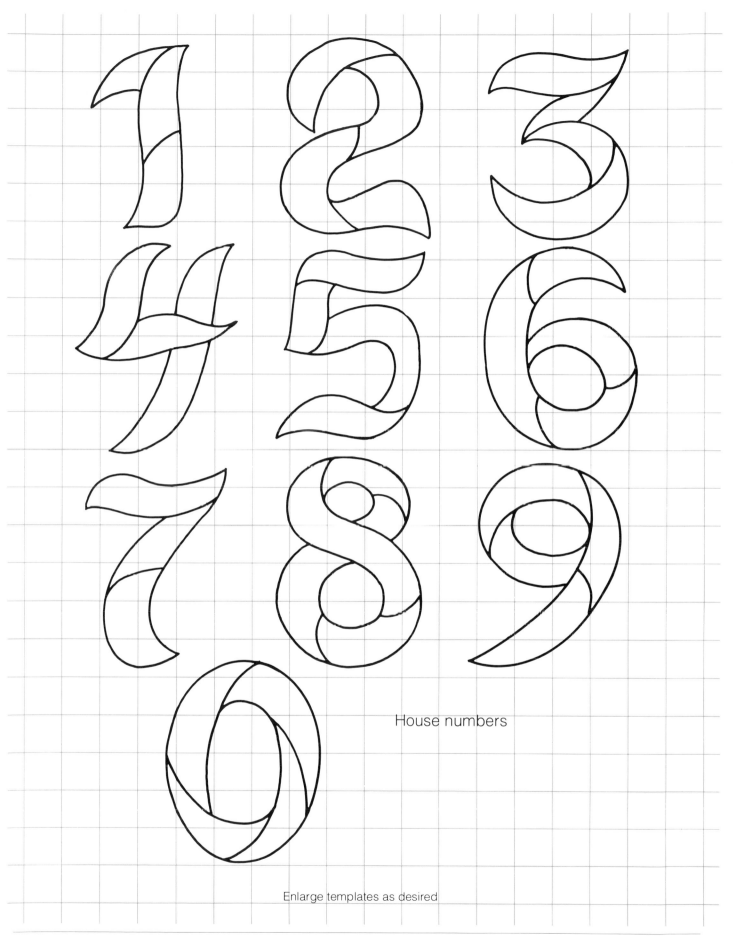

House numbers

Enlarge templates as desired

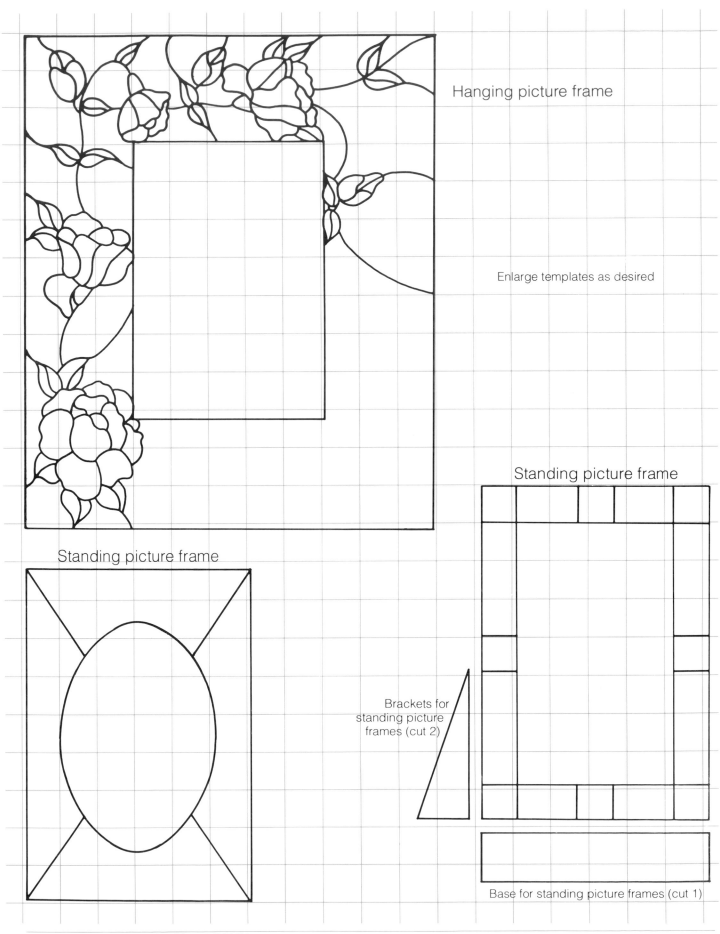

Hanging picture frame

Enlarge templates as desired

Standing picture frame

Standing picture frame

Brackets for
standing picture
frames (cut 2)

Base for standing picture frames (cut 1)

Bird mobile

Full-size templates

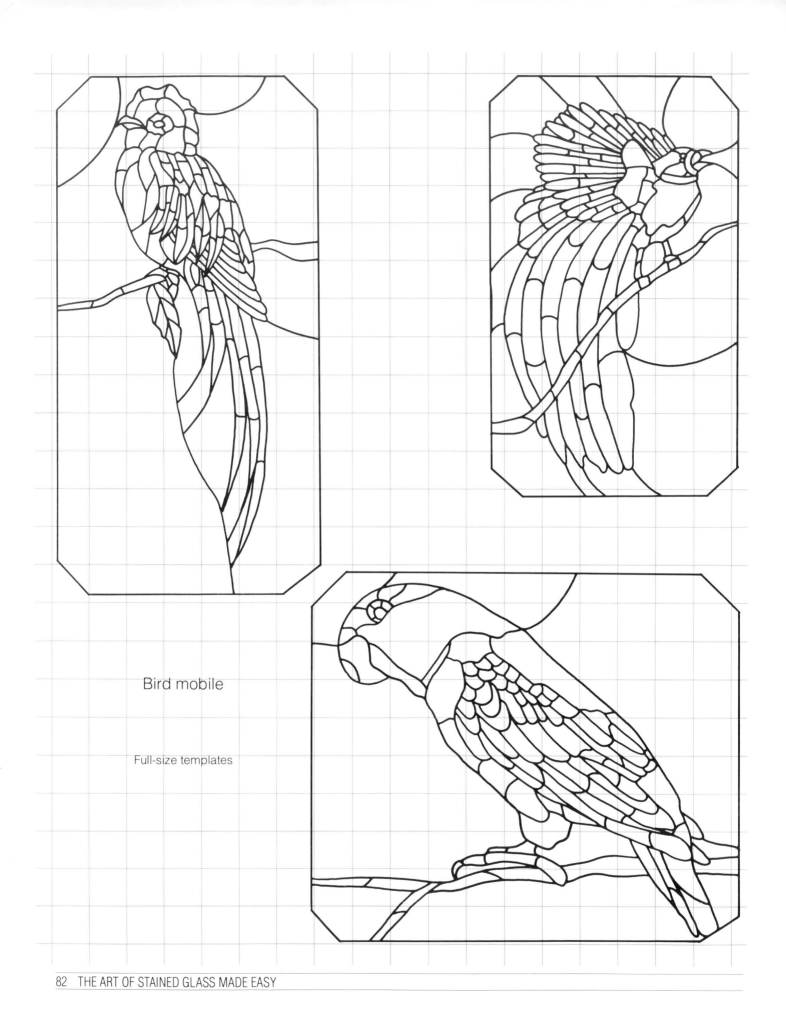

Bird mobile

Full-size templates

Enlarge templates by 25%

Candle light-catcher

Candle light-catcher
(cut 1)

Brackets for corners (cut 4)

(cut 3)

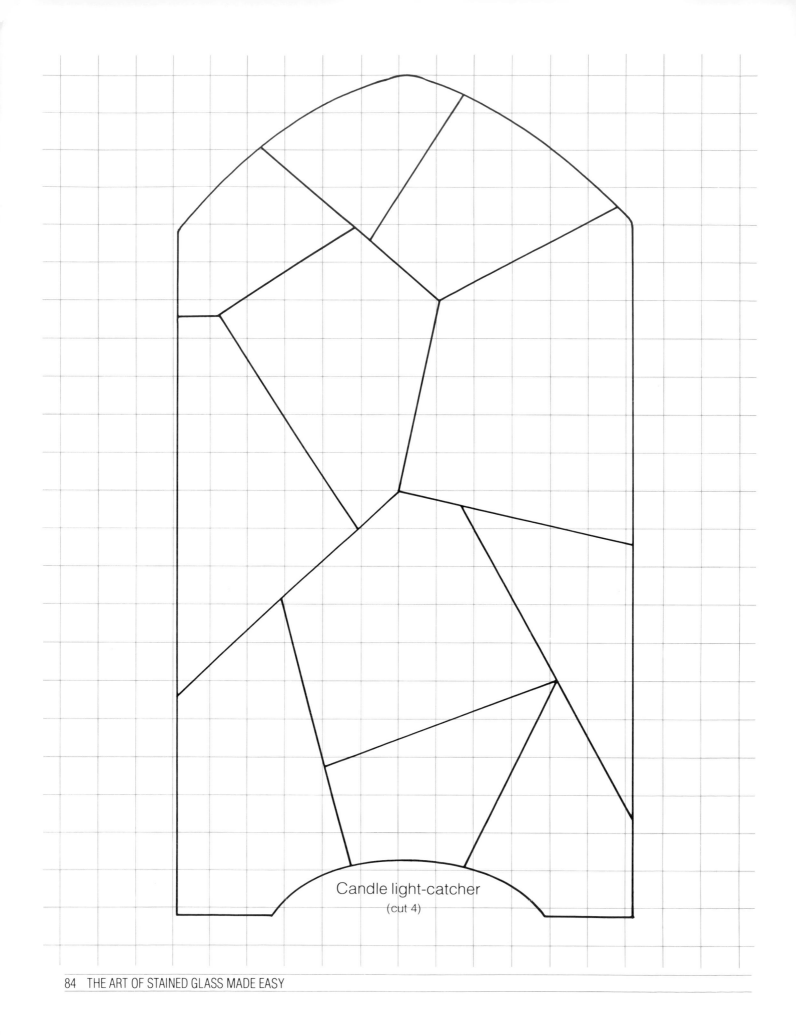

Candle light-catcher
(cut 4)

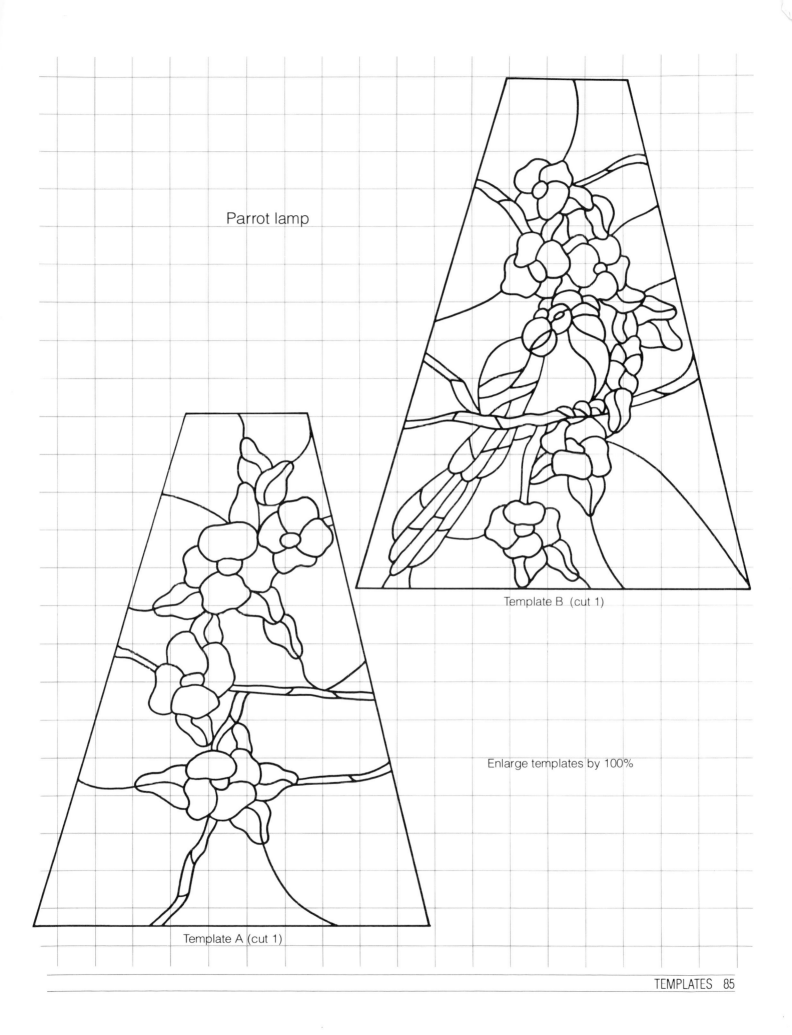

Parrot lamp

Template B (cut 1)

Enlarge templates by 100%

Template A (cut 1)

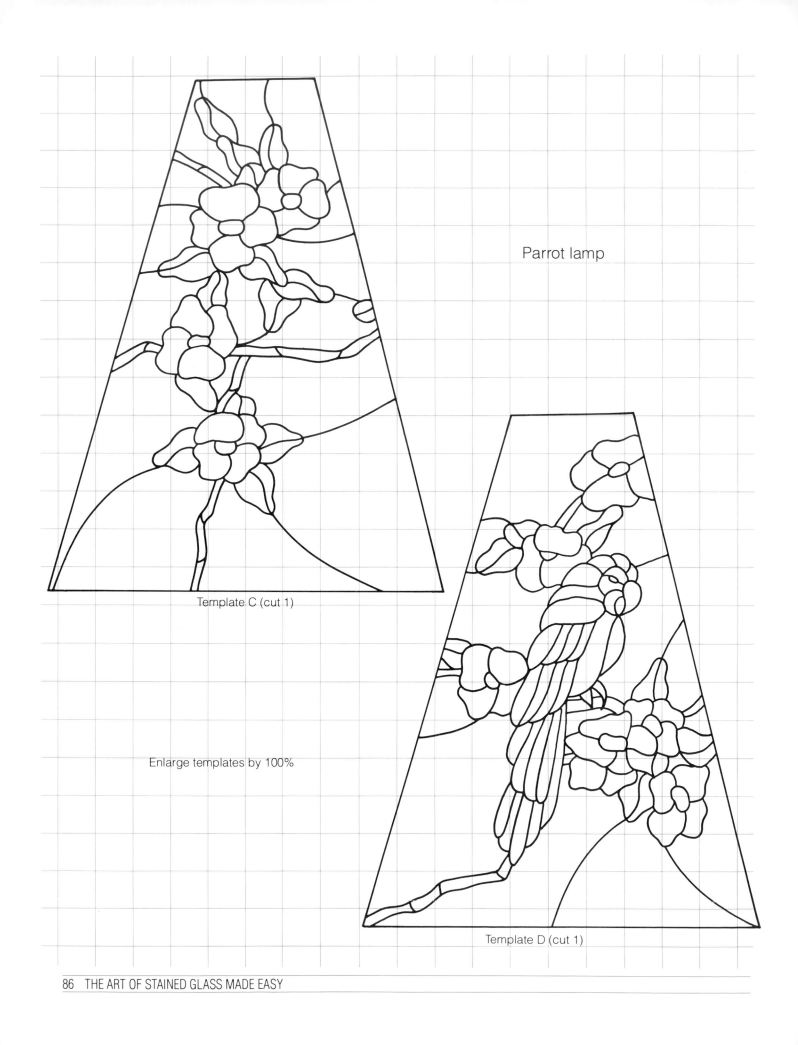

Parrot lamp

Template C (cut 1)

Enlarge templates by 100%

Template D (cut 1)

Parrot lamp

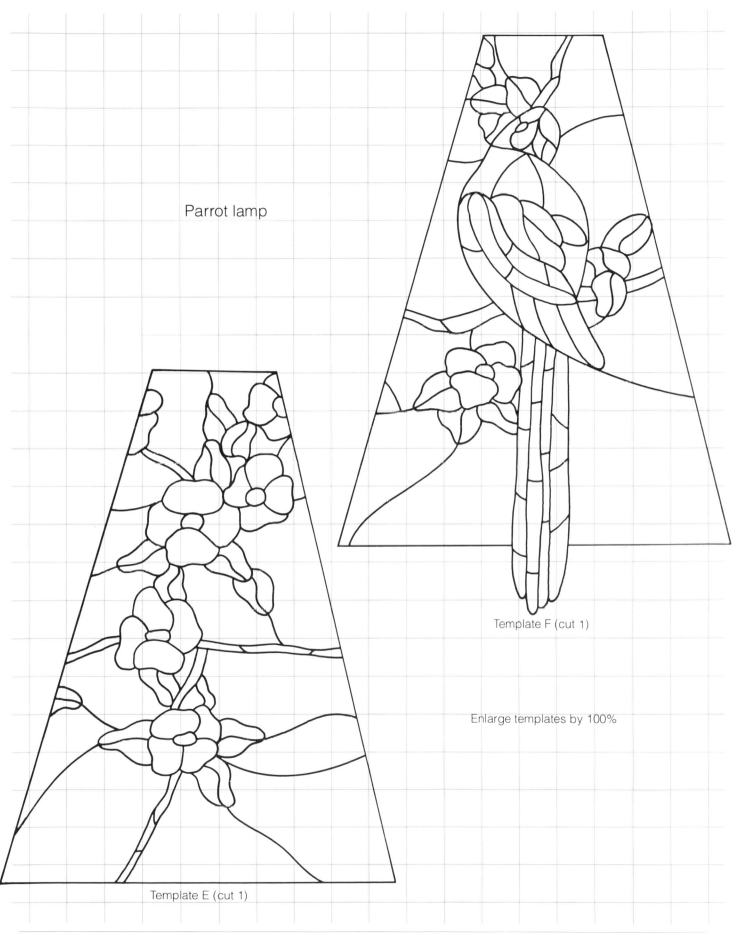

Template F (cut 1)

Enlarge templates by 100%

Template E (cut 1)

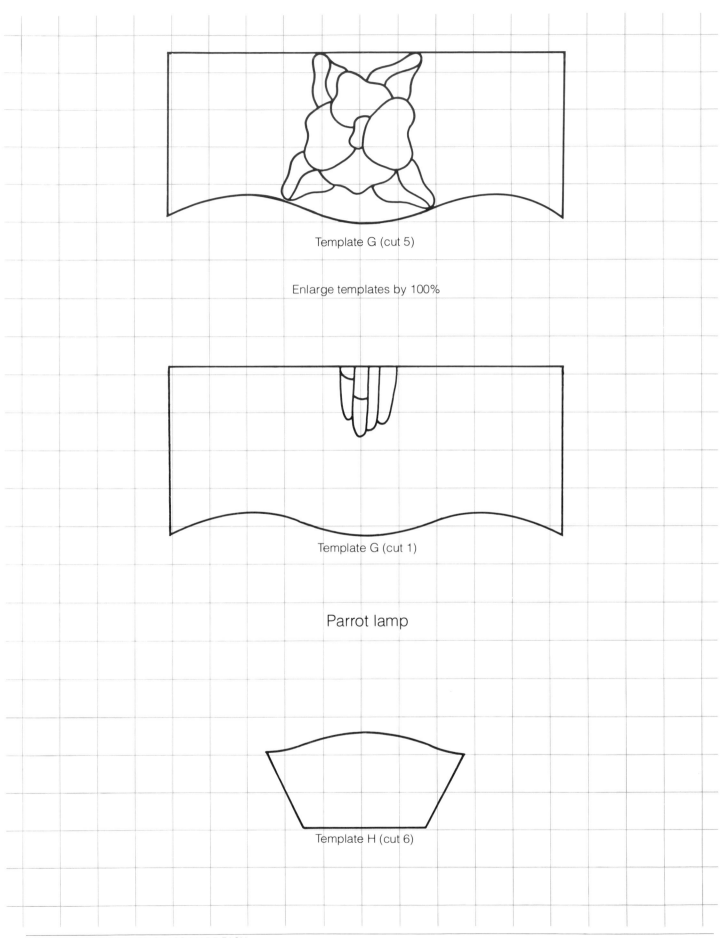

Template G (cut 5)

Enlarge templates by 100%

Template G (cut 1)

Parrot lamp

Template H (cut 6)

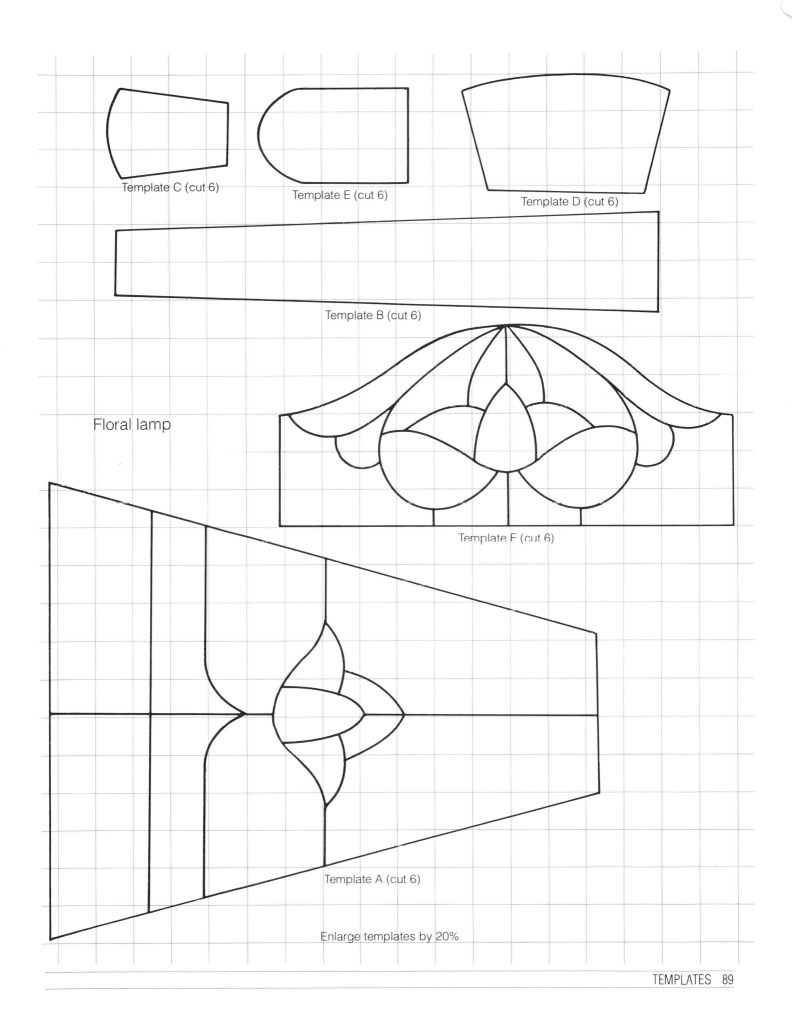

Template C (cut 6)

Template E (cut 6)

Template D (cut 6)

Template B (cut 6)

Floral lamp

Template F (cut 6)

Template A (cut 6)

Enlarge templates by 20%

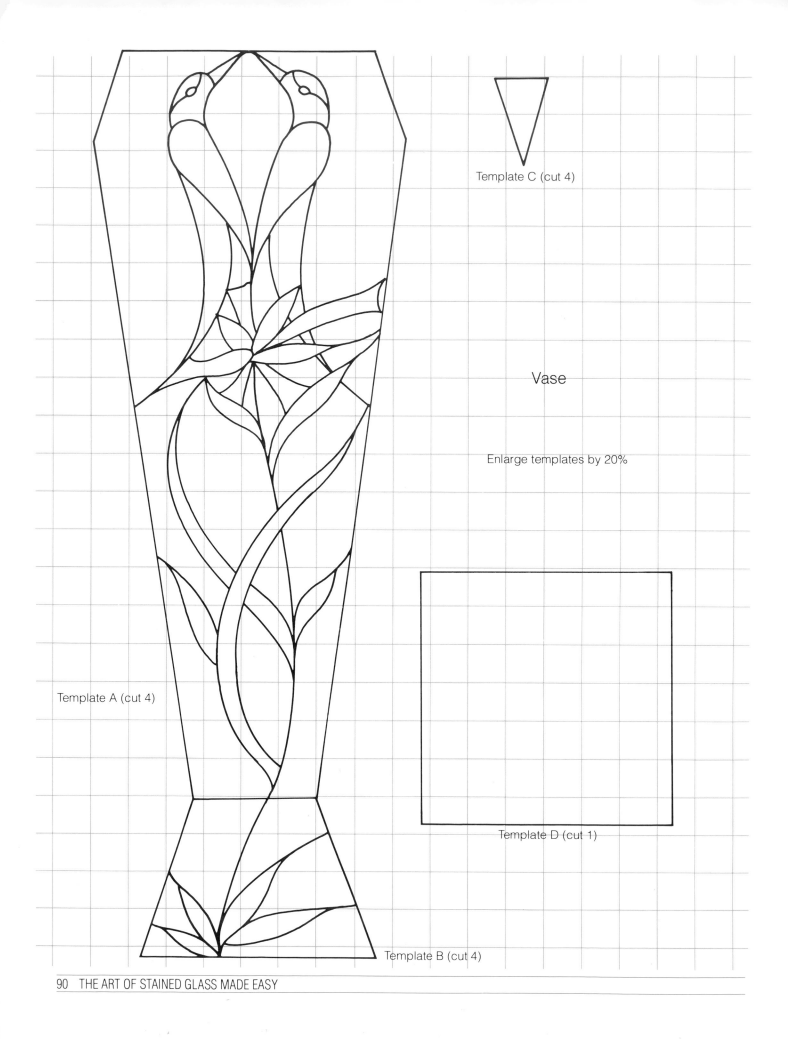

Template C (cut 4)

Vase

Enlarge templates by 20%

Template A (cut 4)

Template D (cut 1)

Template B (cut 4)

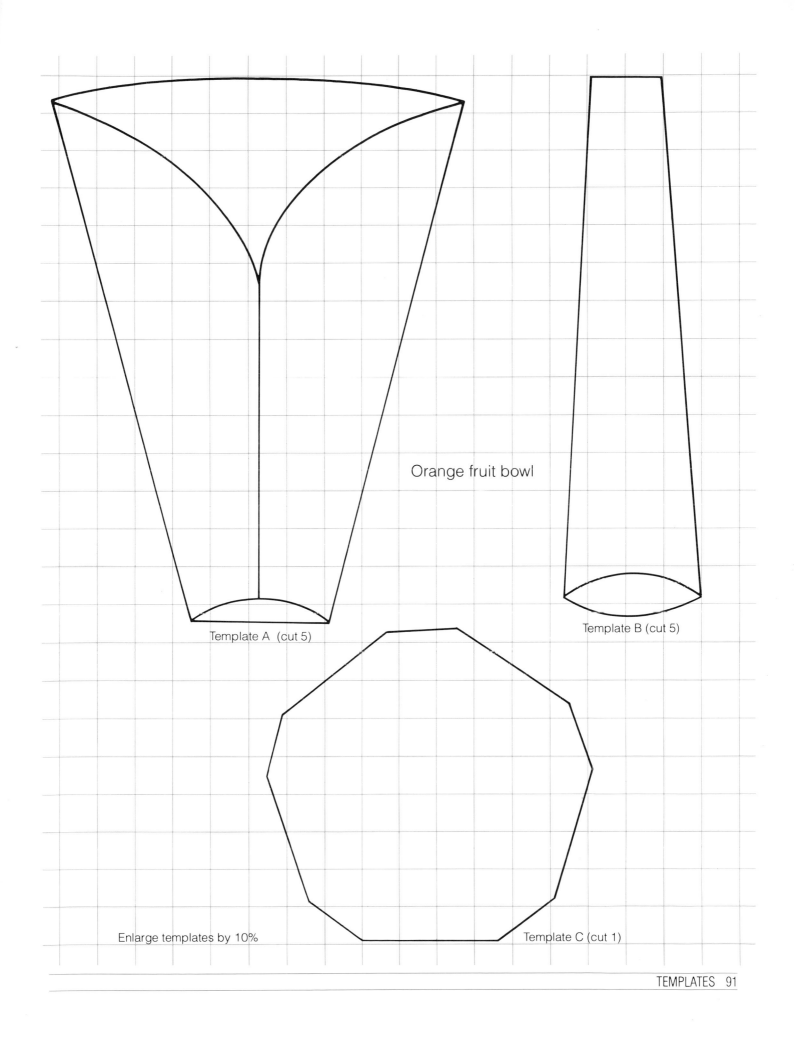

Orange fruit bowl

Template A (cut 5)

Template B (cut 5)

Enlarge templates by 10%

Template C (cut 1)

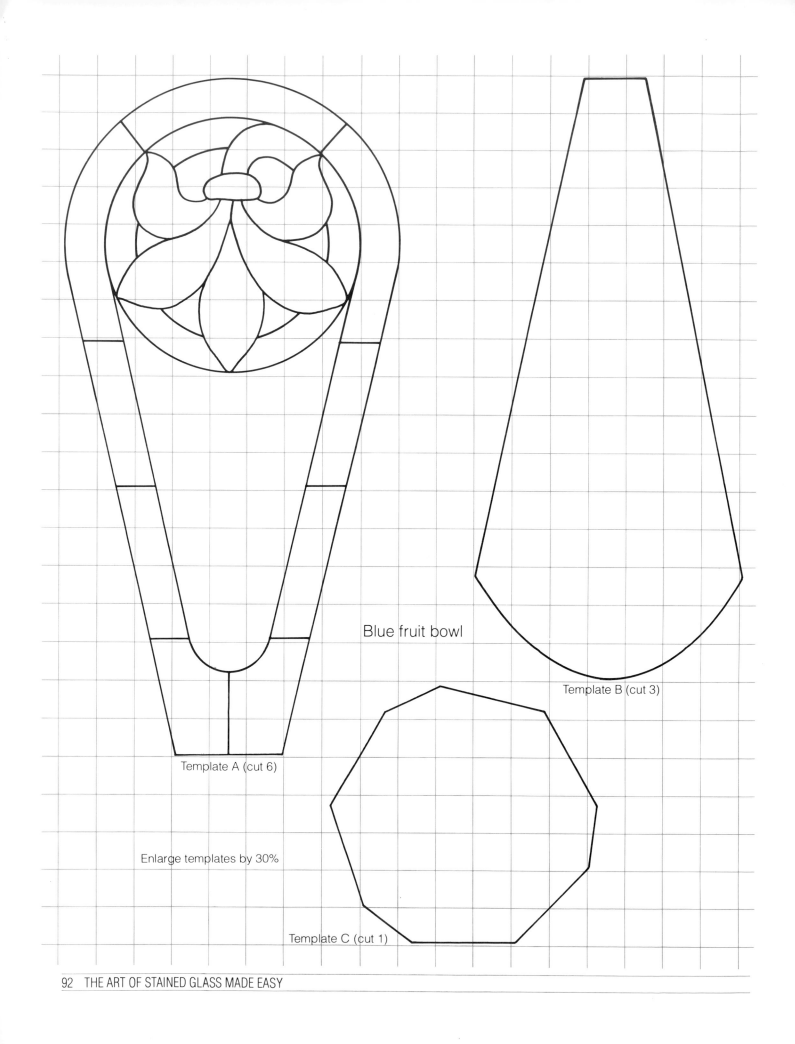

Blue fruit bowl

Template A (cut 6)

Template B (cut 3)

Template C (cut 1)

Enlarge templates by 30%

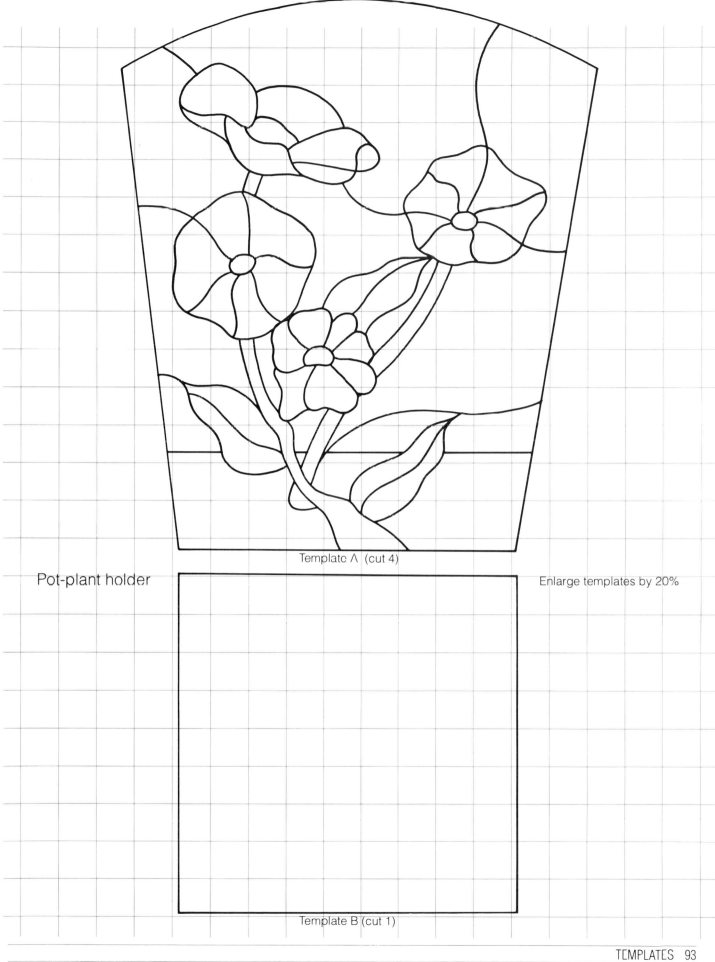

Template A (cut 4)

Pot-plant holder

Enlarge templates by 20%

Template B (cut 1)

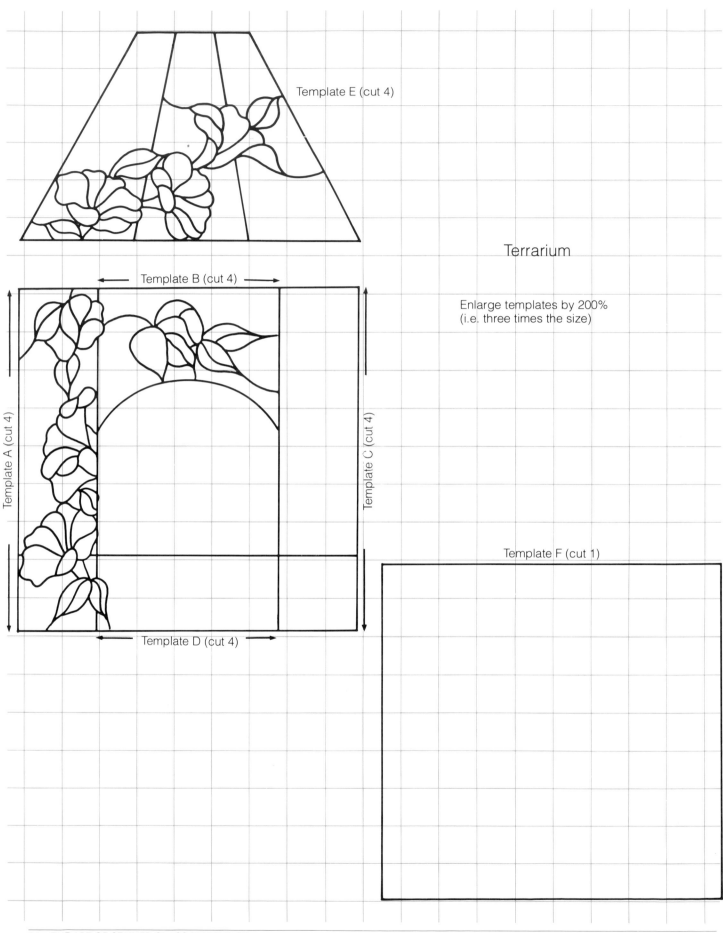

Template E (cut 4)

Terrarium

Enlarge templates by 200%
(i.e. three times the size)

Template B (cut 4)

Template A (cut 4)

Template C (cut 4)

Template D (cut 4)

Template F (cut 1)

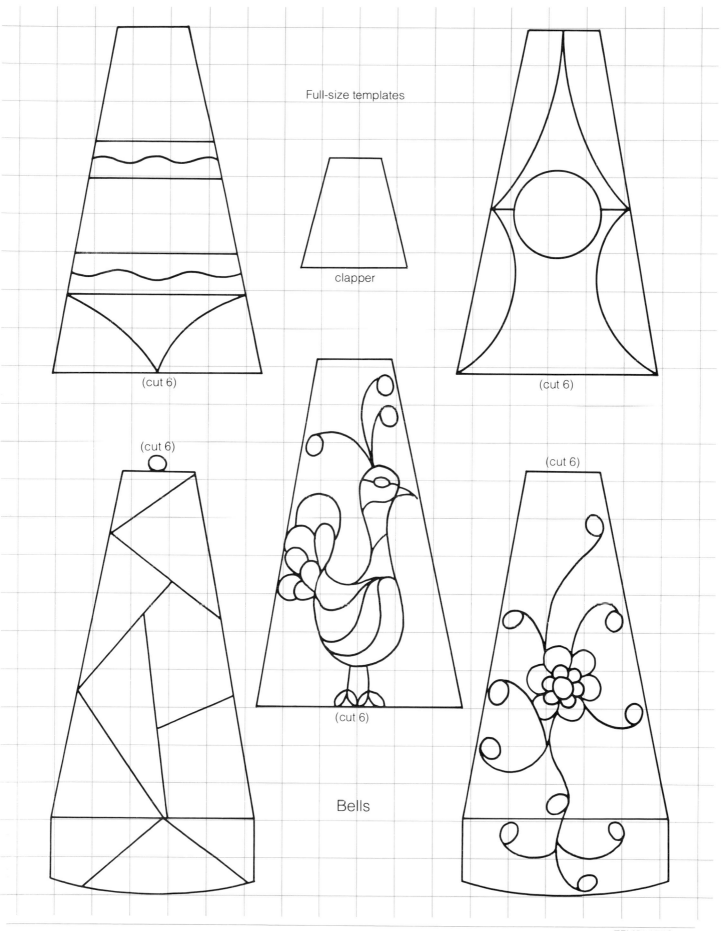

Full-size templates

clapper

(cut 6)

(cut 6)

(cut 6)

(cut 6)

(cut 6)

Bells

STAINED GLASS SUPPLIERS

UNITED KINGDOM

Jennifer Jane Glass Studio
Abbey Studio
Fintray
Aberdeen
Grampian AB2 0JB
Tel: (0224) 791363

Harwil Marketing
Unit 20B Connswater Ind.
   Est.
East Broad Street
Belfast
Northern Ireland BT4 1AN
Tel: (0232) 732311/2

Stained Glass Supplies
Unit 16 Castlefield Ind. Est.
Crossflats
Bingley
W. Yorkshire BD16 2AF
Tel: (0274) 566318

Birmingham Glass
   Studio Ltd
Unit 5
102 Edward Road
Balsall Heath
Birmingham
W. Midlands B12 9LS
Tel: (021) 4400909

Daedalian Glass Ltd
286 Talbot Road
Blackpool
Lancs FY1 3QS
Tel: (0253) 751534

Bournemouth Stained Glass
790 Wimborne Road
Moordown
Bournemouth
Dorset BH9 2DX
Tel: (0202) 514734

Opus Stained Glass
Old Village Hall
Mill Lane
Poynings
Brighton
W. Sussex BN4 7AE
Tel: (0273) 857223

Creative Glass
140d Redland Road
Redland
Bristol
Avon BS6 6YA
Tel: (0272) 737025

Glass House Studio
51 Beckenham Lane
Shortlands Village
Bromley
Kent BR2 0DA
Tel: (081) 464 9793

Cambridge Stained Glass
8 George Street
Willingham
Cambridge
Cambs CB4 5LJ
Tel: (0954) 60301

Ashdowns Ltd
159 Cowbridge Road East
Cardiff
S. Glamorgan CF1 9AH
Tel: (0222) 221573

Edinburgh Stained Glass
   House
46 Balcarres Street
Morningside
Edinburgh
N. Berwick EH10 5JQ
Tel: (031) 452 8062

Leaded Glass Lighting
Unit B
Bakers Boatyard
Brickyard Lane
Starcross
Exeter
Devon EX6 8RY
Tel: (0626) 891383

Stained Glass Supplies Ltd
41 Kingsland Road
East Ham
London E2 8AD
Tel: (071) 874 5661

Stained Glass Construction
   & Design
62 Fairfield Street
Wandsworth
London SW18 1DY
Tel: (071) 874 8822

JWF Ltd
78A Forsyth Road
Newcastle-upon-Tyne
Tyne & Wear NE2 3EU
Tel: (091) 281 0945

Long Eaton Stained Glass
1 Northcote Street
Long Eaton
Notts ND10 1EZ
Tel: (0602) 732320

Broadland Stained Glass
Unit 14
Rowntree Close Ind. Est.
Rowntree Way
Norwich
Norfolk NR7 8SX
Tel: (0603) 401514

Sunrise Stained Glass
58/60 Middle Street
Southsea
Hants P05 4EP
Tel: (0705) 750512

Cheshire Glass Company
Banbury Street
Lower Hillgate
Stockport
Cheshire SK1 3AR
Tel: (061) 480 1873

AUSTRALIA

Adelaide Leadlight Centre
680 South Road
Glandore
SA 5037
Tel: (08) 371 2922

Stained Glass World
929 Burke Road
Camberwell
Victoria 3124
Tel: (03) 882 7962

Spectrum Glass
365 Concord Road
Concord West
NSW 2138
Tel: (02) 743 1201

Tasmanian Stained Glass
16 High Street
Evandale
Tasmania 7212
Tel: (003) 91 8171

The Glass House
8 Romney Street
Kamerunga
Queensland 4870
Tel: (070) 39 2401

The Adelaide Glass Centre
20 College Street
Kent Town
SA 5067
Tel: (08) 363 0766

The Lead Balloon
1240 Malvern Road
Malvern
Victoria 3144
Tel: (03) 822 0686

Tiffany Glass
Corner Harvey and
   Bowman Roads
Marayong
NSW 2148
Tel: (02) 671 6166

Creative Stained Glass and
   Leadline Designs
109 Claisebrook Street
Perth
WA 6000
Tel: (09) 328 1118

The Stained Glass Centre
221 Hale Street
Petrie Terrace
Queensland 4000
Tel: (07) 369 0914

Australian Stained Glass
   Supplies Pty Ltd
39 Pyrmont Street
Pyrmont
NSW 2009
Tel: (02) 660 7424

The Colonial Stained Glass
   Works
220 Subiaco Road
Subiaco
WA 6008
Tel: (09) 381 6255